For Alison
    Who spends her
time in strange places.
        Chuck

GREAT RESORTS OF AMERICA

GREAT RESORTS OF AMERICA

WRITTEN AND PHOTOGRAPHED BY
CHUCK LAWLISS

A WIESER / MARKEL BOOK

HOLT, RINEHART AND WINSTON, New York

Published by Holt, Rinehart and Winston, 383 Madison
Avenue, New York, New York 10017.
Published simultaneously in Canada by
Holt, Rinehart and Winston of Canada, Limited.

Library of Congress Cataloging in Publication Data

Lawliss, Chuck.
  Great resorts of America.
  1. Hotels, taverns, etc.—United States—Directories.
2. Resorts—United States—Directories. I. Title.
TX907.L378 1983   647'.947301   83-8490
ISBN 0-03-063391-5

First Edition

10 9 8 7 6 5 4 3 2 1

Printed in Hong Kong

ISBN 0-03-063391-5

CONTENTS

INTRODUCTION

The twenty-eight resorts featured in this book are marvelously diverse. Some are on the beach while others are in the mountains. Some have pre-Revolutionary roots; others are less than ten years old. Some accommodate more than one thousand guests; others barely one hundred. Some are formal, with string quartets playing at high tea. Many are casual—one has a mariachi band playing at lunch by the swimming pool. Many feature golf and tennis. Some are known for skiing, one for gaming, another for the high road to weight loss. The one quality all share is excellence, a singular ability to please their guests.

There are more resorts in America than in the rest of the world put together. Some four hundred in the United States and Canada have the facilities and the setting to qualify. Nearly one hundred were studied for this book and forty-nine were visited personally. Some of these well deserve the adjective great and the main reason they were not included was the finite amount of space available. There was a deliberate attempt to cover as many resort areas as possible. When all is said and done, however, the choices reflect the author's subjective judgment. Any criticism of the selection should be laid at his door.

It is fitting that there are so many resorts here, for the resort was an American invention, a logical outgrowth of another American invention, the luxury hotel. In Europe, until well into the last century, the rich used private accommodations when they travelled or went on holidays. The rest made do with rather spartan facilities. Such visiting authors as Charles Dickens and Anthony Trollope sang the praises of America's luxury hotels. The late American writer Gene Fowler summed up this phenomenon with an analogy: "The story of Greece is in its temples, that of America is in its hotels."

The history of resorts in America bears examination. The first resorts as such grew up around mineral springs and the prevailing belief that their waters could cure a wide variety of diseases and conditions. Both The Greenbrier and The Homestead began in that fashion. Also shaping the early resorts were the twin constraints of Puritanism and Victorianism—health was an acceptable reason to visit a resort, while pure pleasure most assuredly was not. This reluctance to accept pleasure as a defensible goal lingered into the early 1920s. Mountain and seaside resorts however, were considered healthful alternatives to spending the summer sweltering in the city.

After World War I, resorts enjoyed a boom. American morality relaxed, affluent Americans discovered golf, and railroad companies discovered resorts. Pleasure now was acceptable, and old and new resorts quickly capitalized on golf to attract guests. The railroads found that by building resorts in beautiful wilderness areas, they could build passenger traffic on their lines. The Roaring 20s was a golden age for resorts; seven of the resorts featured in this book were built then.

A characteristic of a great resort is an ability to successfully adapt to change. They weathered the fall from favor of the mineral springs. They stayed a step ahead of the steady improvement in the standard of living by constantly upgrading their rooms, facilities and cuisine. They got through the Depression by catering to the remaining rich, and survived World War II, often by somehow becoming part of the war effort—The Homestead housed interned enemy diplomats, Boca Raton was a barracks for aviation cadets, the Grand Hotel at Point Clear for marines, Sun Valley became a rest and rehabilitation center for battle-weary sailors and marines returning from the Pacific.

One would imagine that a resort's troubles would have ended with the war. However, a procession of new, more complex problems arose. Americans were using their new-found affluence to buy homes in unprecedented numbers. Air conditioning was making summer in the city bearable if not enjoyable. Finally, the growth of airplane travel was giving American resorts stiff competition. Instead of taking the train to a Florida resort for the season, one now flew to an island in the Caribbean. A whirlwind tour of Europe suddenly was more attractive than a leisurely summer in the mountains. By the 1950s, it seemed as if the grand old resorts would fall victim to progress and changing tastes.

Once again, the great resorts showed an uncanny ability to adapt to change. They pulled up their socks, many spending millions in physical improvements. They rid themselves of the old ethnic and racial guest restrictions. The seasonal resorts became year-round resorts. (Of the featured resorts, only the Grand Hotel at Mackinac Island and The Pines at Digby Bay are still seasonal, a condition imposed by their harsh winter weather.) They also found a new patron, one with seemingly limitless means—the American Business Establishment.

A great resort is the perfect place for a corporation to assemble its executives and their wives from around the country, to plan strategy, to reward them for past performance and stimulate them to even greater efforts. A perfect place, too, for business and professional societies and organizations to stage their annual get-togethers. A dentist is much more apt to spend his own money going to a convention at, say, The Breakers than a Chicago hotel, particularly when it is all tax deductible. Since this happy marriage, practically no resort worthy of the name is without a convention or meeting center. Some resorts now are booking meetings and conventions twenty years in advance, such is the demand for prestigious sites. All the great resorts, however, go to great lengths to ensure that their corporate business isn't done at the expense of their social guests. For it is the social guests, especially those who return year after year, who give a great resort its particular character.

Corporation business has provided another boon to the great resorts. The people who come for meetings and conventions often return as social guests. After a sampling of the pleasures of The Broadmoor or The Cloister, it is understandable that one would want to enjoy it at leisure, without the distractions of meetings and business socializing. Once one experiences a great resort, it is easy to become addicted to its many delights.

What is the special appeal of a great resort? First off, the accommodations usually are superb. No hotel, to our knowledge, can match in luxury or comfort the rooms at The Lodge at Pebble Beach or the rental condominiums at Sea Pines Plantation. The food is equally grand, in quality and in presentation. The Shell Room at the Boca Raton Beach Club, the Batik Room at Mauna Kea Beach, and the Orangerie at the Arizona Biltmore are world-class restaurants, even taking into account what a long active day in the sun can do to whet appetites. The physical settings are beyond compare. Dixville

Notch, home of The Balsams, is truly beautiful. So is Lake Tahoe, the setting for Harrah's. There is no happier locale in the Hawaiian Islands than Wailea Beach, no finer view in the Southwest than Sierra Blanca from the Inn of the Mountain Gods. Sun Valley. The Rockies from The Broadmoor. The list goes on and on.

But a great resort is more than rooms, food and setting, however splendid they all are. It is the smorgasbord of activities that is presented to the guest each day that is the true measure of a great resort. A round of golf, perhaps, on a world-famous course. An afternoon of tennis. A few lazy hours on the beach or at the pool. A horseback ride on a wilderness trail. Skiing, snow or water, followed by a sauna and massage. Skeet or lawn bowling. Hang-gliding or croquet. A sightseeing trip to the Grand Canyon in a light plane. Or simply sitting in a rocker on the porch, enjoying a view that is unforgettable. Any or all. Mix or match. No crowds, no lines, no hassle. This is the dimension that makes great resorts so special.

This book is an attempt to capture in words and pictures the essential quality of these resorts, something of their histories, something of the qualities that make each of them what it is. If the book is successful, a reader familiar with a resort will think, "Yes. That's the way I remember it." An unfamiliar reader will think, "This is a place I'd really like to visit."

Those who are stimulated to the second response will find in the appendix the information necessary to start planning a great resort holiday. Rates and dates are constantly changing, of course, but those quoted were up-to-date at press time, and, certainly, are good for comparative purposes. The prudent will be rewarded by a study of such things as off-season rates and packages that fit their particular interests.

This book was a labor of love. We spent more than six months visiting resorts, seeing old friends and making new ones. The resorts, individually and collectively, have left an indelible impression and a longing to return. Our wish is that you enjoy the book, and that the book will be a prelude to enjoying the resorts themselves.

GRAND HOTEL

Mackinac Island

The Grand Hotel at Mackinac Island: Queen of the Summer Hotels (overleaf). The front lawn rolls gently down to the swimming pool and Lake Huron (opposite). A carriage approaches the hotel (above left). Autos are not permitted on the island. White rocking chairs wait at attention for guests on the 880-foot front porch (far left). The lake is a bit chilly for swimming even in July but the hotel pool seems most adequate to the task of refreshing guests.

GRAND HOTEL

Lake Michigan and Lake Huron meet at the historic Straits of Mackinac, a name borrowed and shortened from the Indian word "Michilimackinac," meaning great turtle. Indeed, Mackinac Island, barely east of the straits, does resemble a great turtle. Father Jacques Marquette established a mission in 1671 on the nearby mainland, and by 1715 the French had built Fort Michilimackinac. After the British defeated the French, the fort was moved to the heights of Mackinac Island. The area was ceded to the United States after the Revolution but the British recaptured the fort in the War of 1812. After the war, the fort was strengthened and guarded the northern frontier until about 1840.

Mackinac Island was the headquarters of John Jacob Astor's fur empire until the trappers had made the beaver virtually extinct in the Great Lakes region. From the 1840s to the 1880s, fishing supported the economy of Mackinac Island but, like the beaver,

the trout and whitefish finally became too sparse to support an industry. The islanders then turned to the two resources that were inexhaustible—natural beauty and the glorious summer weather.

Tourists had been coming to Mackinac Island since the 1820s and the few waterfront hotels were inadequate to meet the demand. The island was designated a national park in 1875—only Yellowstone, created in 1872, is older—and the flow of visitors increased. Under the leadership of Francis B. Stockbridge, a businessman and later a U.S. Senator, plans for a grand hotel were drawn up. Financed by the Michigan Central Railroad, the Grand Rapids & Indiana, and the Detroit & Cleveland Navigation Company, an elegant structure was built of Michigan pine on the heights overlooking the straits. The Grand Hotel opened on July 10, 1887, and among the first guests were the Potter Palmers, the Marshall Fields, the Armours, the Swifts, and the Adolphus

11

The honeymoon suite has a magnificient view should one choose to look at it (left). A violinist is as much a part of high tea as a lemon slice (opposite above). Pretty maids all in a row (opposite below left). A view toward the main dining room. Note the undulation in the floor, inevitable in a huge, century-old frame building. The carpet pattern is trellised geraniums, symbol of the Grand Hotel.

Busches. The hotel was a success and soon the cream of Midwest society was building summer homes on the island. In 1901, one of the wealthy summer residents asked permission of the park commission to bring his new motor car to the island. The commission decided against the request and banned all automobiles—a ruling that remains in force today.

An interesting nine-hole, 2,710-yard, par-34 golf course winds across the hillside. Also available on the 500 acres are four tennis courts, the magnificent serpentine swimming pool down the lawn from the front of the hotel, horses and miles of bridle paths, bicycling, shuffleboard and a Vita-Course exercise trail. A must during one's stay is a carriage tour of the island.

Evening is the nicest time of the day at Mackinac. Strolling on the front lawn as shadows lengthen and the lights come on in the hotel, the Grand sparkles like an ocean liner at sea. For a brief time, it is the Golden Age again. And every guest becomes a part of it.

Over the years, the Grand Hotel was often full but rarely profitable. Expenses were high and the season was only two months long. In the early 1900's, the hotel was extended 300 feet, a fifth story of rooms added, and a golf course built. Later under still another ownership, a swimming pool and a patio garden were built and the main building refurbished. Prosperity didn't come to the Grand, however, until the advent of a young man named W. Stewart Woodfill. Woodfill started as a desk clerk in 1919 and by 1923 was named manager. Ten years later he owned the hotel. Under his leadership the season was extended to six months, the aristocratic tone of the resort was established once and for all, and the Grand became pre-eminent among summer hotels. The Grand, now owned by the R. D. Mussers, has lost none of its luster since.

Visiting the Grand Hotel is a unique experience, one that begins the moment one steps off the ferry from St. Ignace. A top-hatted, red-coated coachman with a Victorian carriage drives the guests up the hill to the hotel, with the golf course and gardens on one side, the view of the straits on the other. Under the portico are liveried doormen, up the stairs is the magnificent Parlor. Pause a moment before entering and admire the longest porch in the world. Its 880 feet are dotted with comfortable wooden rockers from which to enjoy the spectacular view, its length lined with flower boxes filled with more than 5,000 geraniums, the hotel's emblem.

The interior is equally splendid. In 1977, interior designer Carleton Varney was asked by the Mussers to redecorate the public rooms, a project that was quickly expanded to encompass the entire hotel. Now it is both charming and radiant in daffodil yellow, sky blue and deep green. The carpets incorporate the geranium emblem in a trellis pattern. The grounds and the interiors are in harmony at the Grand.

While the redecoration was going on, the hotel was somewhat enlarged and 9 steel pillars were installed to replace the original supporting cedar logs. Nevertheless, one of the charms of this wooden Greek Revival building is that there probably aren't two parallel lines in it; to look down any corridor is to see the undulation of the floor. Also new is the electronically controlled sprinkler system, one of the largest and most sophisticated in the world.

Through the years the Grand Hotel has played host to Presidents Grover Cleveland, William Howard Taft and Theodore Roosevelt. Mrs. Lyndon B. Johnson was the guest of honor at a 1964 reception. Gerald Ford addressed a Republican breakfast here. Mark Twain visited. So did Julius Rosenwald, Chauncey Depew and General George Catlett Marshall. "This Time For Keeps" with Esther Williams and Jimmy Durante was filmed here. More recently, the hotel was the setting for the movie "Somewhere in Time," starring Christopher Reeve.

A pillared walkway leads to the main dining room where all the guests may be accommodated at one sitting. The six-course dinner is outstanding: smoked Nova Scotia salmon, prosciutto princess, or supreme of shrimps; Indian corn chowder, gazpacho, or chilled banana-strawberry soup, a choice of salads; broiled filet of Mackinac whitefish, honey-glazed duckling with wild rice and a peppercorn sauce, or prime rib of beef with vegetables, topped off with a Grand pecan ball, strawberries Romanoff, or carrot cake. A grand buffet is presented each day at luncheon.

After dinner, guests may have demitasse and liqueurs in the Parlor, or go dancing in the Terrace Room. A short walk away is the Grand Stand, overlooking the golf course, where a piano bar keeps going until the wee hours. The Grand is strictly modified American Plan and no tipping is allowed. Coats and ties are de rigeur after six p.m.

AUBERGE

GRAY ROCKS

AUBERGE GRAY ROCKS

In the Laurentians, a small mountain chain north of Montreal, winter comes early and stays late, and skiing is closer to being a religion than a sport. There is no finer skiing in the Laurentians than at Gray Rocks, no more comfortable place to stay, and no finer ski school anywhere on the continent. In the early 1930's, a rope tow was installed on Sugar Peak near the inn. A modern ski lift came ten years later, about the time that some of Europe's top ski professionals arrived seeking refuge from the war. At the Snow Eagle Ski School they helped evolve the Modern Ski Technique, taught almost universally. One measure of the quality of the ski school is this: at capacity, the inn can accommodate 500 guests; there are 50 instructors in the ski school. With modern snow-making techniques, the ski season here is five months long. The mountain now has three double chair lifts, two T-bars and 18 runs.

It all began with George Ernest Wheeler, who came to this part of French Canada in 1890 and built a sawmill, which led to a profitable construction business. Many of his friends would find excuses to visit him, and enjoy the hunting and fishing in the mountains. In the early 1900's forest fires devastated the area and the dreams of Mr. Wheeler and his wife, Lucile. Reluctant to leave, they opened the inn in 1906. The inn has been owned and operated by the Wheeler family ever since.

Though skiing is king, the inn is busy year round. It is situated on the shores of Lac Ouimet, the grounds cover 2,000 lovely acres, and there is a variety of activities in every season. The golf course—6,455 yards, par 72—dates back to 1922 and is the oldest in the area. There are 22 Har Tru tennis courts, and the tennis school, run by Butch Staples in association with Dennis Van der Meer, was rated by *World Tennis* as one of the best values anywhere. There is swimming in a pool or the lake, sailing canoeing, water skiing, fishing, riding, lawn bowling, hiking, cookouts and a full range of supervised activities for youngsters. For indoor sports there is a piano bar and nightly dancing. There is an air strip and seaplane facility for private pilots a few minutes from the inn. A seaplane may be engaged for a sightseeing flight.

Gray Rocks has a French flair. The staff is bilingual but some of the guests are not, which may lead to minor problems in socializing. An English-speaking young man trying to charm a French mademoiselle here has a delightful task in store. This French flair, however, pays dividends in the dining room. La soupe aux pois à la Canadienne, l'entrecôte de boeuf au poivre, flambé au cognac, les cuisses de grenouilles provencale, les poires flambées au pernod, and l'omelette Alaska flambee au Marasquin are merely highlights of a distinguished menu.

In 1970, Gray Rocks acquired Le Chateau, a smaller but equally attractive lodge, on the lake less than a mile from the inn. The dining rooms and lounges are intimate and offer a nice change of pace. Like Gray Rocks, Le Chateau is on the American Plan and offers good value, particularly to Americans enjoying the favorable rate of exchange.

Indian legend tells of a god that lives in the mountains here and makes the earth tremble when he is disturbed. He must share the guests' high opinion of Gray Rocks for the earth hasn't trembled here in years.

17

THE PINES

THE PINES

DIGBY BAY, NOVA SCOTIA

To a gourmet, Nova Scotia is synonymous with salmon, and Digby Bay with scallops, for both are arguably the best in the world. To a traveler, Nova Scotia is perhaps the most charming and picturesque area in North America, and The Pines at Digby Bay a perfect base for a Nova Scotian holiday. An historian might note that Nova Scotia was the key to English Canada, and that Port Royal Habitation, a restoration of the 1605 settlement a few minutes drive from The Pines, was the earliest permanent settlement north of St. Augustine, Florida. A naturalist would point out that the Bay of Fundy and Annapolis Bay have the greatest tidal bores in the world, rising in some places to 40 feet and more. Those of Scottish descent should revel in the fact that Nova Scotia is practically as Scottish as Scotland itself. Queen Elizabeth personally opened the International Gathering of the Clans here in 1979. And doesn't every schoolchild recall Longfellow's epic "Evangeline," the tale of young French lovers separated when they and their families were expelled by the British from Acadia, as Nova Scotia once was called?

There is, indeed, something for everyone here, even those who simply want to relax. Beyond anything else, The Pines is relaxing. The view across the landscaped grounds and the bay is as soothingly beautiful as a lullabye. The view from the veranda of the village and the fishing fleet seems to roll back time to a gentler age. History is important to an understanding of the ethos of this place. Port Royal fell to a British fleet early in the conquest of French Canada and was renamed Annapolis, "Anne's City," after Queen Anne. Digby Bay was named after Admiral Robert Digby who brought 1,500 Loyalist settlers here after the American Revolution, among whom was the great-greatfather of Thomas

Edison. The first Pines Hotel was built in 1903 and was pressed into service as a Canadian Army officers' billet during World War I. The Canadian Pacific Railway bought the hotel in 1919, tore it down ten years later and built the present four-story French-Norman chateau, containing 90 guest rooms. Later, 31 cottages were added, each with a fireplace in the living room, several bedrooms, and porches overlooking the bay. Since 1965, the resort has been owned and operated, quite skillfully, by the province.

The Scottish game of golf is played on a challenging 18-hole, par-71 course. The par-three, 178-yard second hole with a large pond athwart the fairway, was named one of the most picturesque and challenging holes in the country by Canadian golf writers. On the 285-yard uphill 11th, the first man to drive the green was a guest who had made a name for himself in another sport—Babe Ruth. Rounding out the recreational facilities are a putting green on the front lawn, two lighted tennis courts, a glass-enclosed, heated swimming pool, shuffleboard courts, and a croquet court. Sailing on the bay and superb deep-sea fishing can be arranged.

Broiled scallops are hawked in town by sidewalk vendors as taffy is in Atlantic City. In the dining room at The Pines, scallops are treated more imaginatively: a casserole of maritime scallops is an especially good example. Lobsters, salmon, haddock, halibut—all are caught locally and cooked to perfection. A particular treat is the traditional fisherman's breakfast: a brown, crusty, rib-sticking chicken-and-potato concoction called Rappie Pie.

The Pines is one of the last great summer resorts, closing from October through May, when Nova Scotia is left to those made of sterner stuff. The all too brief summer, however, is more than sufficient to provide wonderful memories for many a long winter.

THE BALSAMS

As clouds roll in to fill Dixville Notch two guests walk back to the hotel (overleaf). A chair on the front lawn is both relaxing and a sure way not to miss anything (left above). The fleet's in as a long afternoon draws to a close (left). The lake is stocked with rainbow trout and the kitchen will prepare your catch for dinner. The golf course (opposite) was designed by Donald Ross in the early 1900's to take advantage of the remarkable terrain. From the club house one can see Vermont, New Hampshire, Canada and, except for a mountain in the way, Maine.

THE BALSAMS

At the turn of the century, much of New England was dotted with grand resort hotels, and together they helped define the elegance of the Victorian Age. But fire, neglect, and changing times have claimed all but a handful. The best example extant of the glory that once was is the The Balsams, a big, rambling hotel with turrets and seemingly endless towers that looks across a small lake to the awesome slopes that form the northernmost pass in the White Mountains. The first owner of this land was the Dix family, and the first settlers are buried nearby. They were among America's first innkeepers, providing food and lodging for travelers going through the notch.

The Balsams was built in 1873, expanded in 1916, and, has since added the swimming pool, and downhill ski complex. The resort includes 15,000 acres, enough for a small kingdom which in many ways it is. It owns its own telephone company; it uses waste wood from the forests to produce its own electricity and winter heat. There are 232 rooms in the hotel, all comfortably appointed. The public rooms are spacious, most with well-used fireplaces. There is a library with vintage books, and a billiard room. A lobby plaque notes that Theodore Roosevelt and Warren G. Harding were among its distinguished guests. It is a tribute to The Balsams that such a historical footnote comes as no surprise.

There are two golf courses, a nine-hole, 2,005-yard, par 32 executive course, the Coashaukee, and an 18-hole championship course, the Panorama, 6,525 yards, par 72, built in 1912. From it one can see New Hampshire, Vermont, Canada, and, except for a mountain in the way, Maine. Its tea-cup sand traps and convex greens are hallmarks of its distinguished designer, Donald Ross.

A full dozen chefs present their delicious handiwork (opposite) Looking back from Dixville Notch, The Balsams resembles a Ruritanian castle. (left). In Colonial days, the notches of New Hampshire permitted travel to and from Canada. The lake catches the fire of autumn leaves.

Other facilities include three clay and three plexi-cushion tennis courts, a heated swimming pool, volleyball, bicycling, horseshoes, croquet, bocci, badminton, and a profusion of hiking trails. Paddleboats, rowboats and canoes are available at the lake along with fishing gear. The lake is stocked with lake and rainbow trout, no license is required, and the kitchen will prepare your catch for dinner.

In the winter come the skiers. The hotel's Wilderness Ski Area is minutes away with a 4,000-foot double chairlift and two T-bars, twelve trails up to two miles in length, a cozy base lodge, and an excellent ski school. There are miles of cross-country trails, a network of snowmobile trails, ice skating, tobogganing, and snow-shoeing. The mean annual snowfall is in excess of 200 inches.

The Balsams is one of the few resorts that is strictly American Plan, and here it means more than simply "meals included."

There are no extra greens fees, no ski lift charges, no boat rentals at the lake. The food is both abundant and excellent. A grand buffet is served at luncheon. Dinner brings such specialities as veal Oscar, baked stuffed shrimp, and succulent prime ribs. After dinner, there is live entertainment in either the Ballroom or the Wilderness Lounge.

One room at The Balsams has been seen by more Americans than probably any other hotel room in the world. In presidential primaries, the few enfranchised voters of Dixville Notch gather in the Ballot Room and cast their votes at the stroke of midnight. Network television cameras watch as the ballots are counted moments later and the results announced—the first 're-turns in the country's first primary. Good fun, this brief moment in the media spotlight, but Dixville Notch has a more solid claim to fame: the quality and charm of The Balsams.

HERSHEY

Pennsylvania Dutch cuisine makes a tempting display (overleaf). The hotel's formal garden attracts thousands of visitors each year (opposite). Century-old Apostolic Clock is a highlight at the Hershey Museum of American Life (far left). Wooden doors open and Apostles circle in front of the figure of Jesus. A statue of Mr. Hershey and orphan boy is in the rotunda of the Milton Hershey School (left). He founded and financed school for orphans and other needy children.

HOTEL HERSHEY

Guests checking in at the Hotel Hershey are given bars of chocolate, for chocolate is what Hershey is all about. It was in a cornfield here that Milton Hershey, "The Father of the Chocolate Bar," built his factory and the model community for his workers that later bore his name. The main streets in Hershey are Chocolate and Cocoa avenues, and the streetlights are shaped like Hershey Kisses. At Hershey's Chocolate World, an automated ride takes you through the story of chocolate from cacao bean plantations to the finished product. Hersheypark is a theme park where one is greeted by people dressed as chocolate bars. And the factory permeates the air with the aroma of chocolate.

From the beginning, Mr. Hershey wanted a grand hotel for his town. He and his wife admired the Heliopolis Hotel in Cairo, and he purchased the original plans only to find the construction estimates astronomical. Instead he gave his architect a picture postcard of a Mediterrean hotel, saying he wanted "something like that." What he got when it was completed in 1933 was a masterpiece of Spanish architecture, "a palace," said Lowell Thomas, "that outpalaces the palaces of the Maharajahs of India." "Other men have yachts to play with," Mr. Hershey once explained. "The hotel is my yacht."

His personal touches are much in evidence. He wanted the hotel to have a Spanish patio, tiled floors, and a fountain. They are there. And he wanted a dining room with a good view from every table. "In some places," he said, "if you don't tip well, they put you in a corner." The lovely, semi-circular dining room with 13 magnificent stained-glass windows has no corners.

The public rooms are high-ceilinged and attractively formal,

the 250 guest rooms and six suites are comfortable and well appointed. Dining at Hershey is a particular pleasure. The guest may savor traditional continental cuisine, and, from time to time, specialities from the surrounding Pennsylvania Dutch countryside. Nor is the sportsman neglected: five golf courses totaling 72 holes are nearby. Hershey is known as "The Golf Capital of Pennsylvania." Also available are tennis courts, indoor and outdoor swimming pools, a riding stable with a rare Chincoteague pony, and hiking and cross-country ski trails.

On the resort's 90 acres are six of the finest gardens to be found anywhere. The complex includes: the Fountain Garden, home of the famous statue, "Boy With the Leaking Boot;" the English Formal Garden with its geometric shape, and recurring patterns of hemlock and red leaf barberry; the Colonial Garden, an imaginative presentation of flowers, perennial shrubs, and herbs; the Rock Garden; the Japanese Garden with a waterfall cascading into a pond crossed by three bridges; and The Italian garden with classic statuary and columns. Tens of thousands visit the Hershey Gardens each year.

A holiday in Hershey should include two other stops. The Hershey Museum of American Life has a fine collection of Pennsylvania Dutch and American Indian artifacts. And the Milton Hershey School, founded and funded by Milton Hershey. Since 1909, it has grown into an outstanding plant on 10,000 acres providing a home and education for orphans and other children from four to 16 who were not receiving adequate parental care. The school, more than the hotel or, perhaps, even chocolate itself, was closest to Milton Hershey's heart.

31

THE

HOMESTEAD

The stately old Homestead looks on as a golfer lines up a chip shot (overleaf). The tower has been the symbol of this resort for more than a century (opposite). Sunlight streams into a guest lounge (left) and plays patterns across the quarry slate floor. Ironically, Japanese diplomats were interned in this bastion of Southern hospitality after Pearl Harbor.

THE HOMESTEAD

On a crisp fall morning the mist rising from the hot springs can blur a guest's view of this magnificent resort, just as the passage of time has blurred its beginnings. Indians, it is believed, were bathing in the healing waters here as early as 1600. In 1750, a medical missionary, Dr. Thomas Walker, happened by the springs on his way to Kentucky, and found six invalids bathing in the water. He noted in his journal "The spring is very clear and warmer than new milk." The first hotel was built here in 1766 by Commodore Thomas Bullitt who had been assigned to nearby Fort Dinwiddie by George Washington. He named the hotel The Homestead and it stood a long time. It was acquired in 1832 by Dr. Thomas Goode who improved the bathhouses and inaugurated a "spout bath" that is still in use. Business flourished at the spa and Dr. Goode built a new hotel in 1846 on the site of the present resort. The new hotel was wooden, with a long columned porch. It had no plumbing other than a few public toilets. Open fires provided heat, oil lamps light. After Dr. Goode's death in 1858, the hotel languished until near the end of the century.

A group of executives of the Chesapeake & Ohio Railroad bought The Homestead in 1890 and soon a C & O branch line was built to Hot Springs. (The Homestead now has its own airport, Ingalls Field, about 17 miles away.) A modern spa was soon in operation, incorporating the latest techniques of European spas, and ten cottages were built near the hotel. In 1892, a golf course of sorts was opened. More and more guests were coming to The Homestead, but in the summer of 1901 a fire broke out in the bakery and the hotel burned to the ground in three hours. The owners moved immediately to rebuild.

To see The Homestead today, it is hard to imagine that the red-brick, Georgian-style building was not designed by one man and built all at one time. Rather, the architectural firm of Elzner & Anderson designed the main section, built in 1902, and the west wing, in 1903. In 1914, the west wing was built, designed by the same firm. The Garden Room, Ballroom, Empire Room and Theatre were added in 1921. In 1929, the white clock tower was added, designed by Charles D. Wetmore of Warren & Wetmore. Despite the time lapse and the change of architects, the hotel has a marvelous structural unity.

The Cascades Golf Course (6,566 yards, par 70) was opened in 1924. Its architect, William S. Flynn, then redesigned the course at The Homestead and expanded it to 18 holes. The club house at The Cascades was originally the hideaway of a stock market speculator named Jakey Rubino. Mr. Rubino tried to corner the market of the National Cordage Company and failed. He was wiped out and The Homestead acquired his property. A third course was added in 1963, the challenging Lower Cascades Course, a 6,726 yard, par 72, design by Robert Trent Jones.

In the 1930's there was another course, the Goat Course, where Homestead caddies played. A young caddy named Samuel Jackson Snead first played golf here before going on to fame. He is now a member of The Homestead staff, and his home is near The Cascades. "The Cascades is the finest course in the South," says the old master Snead, who recently carded a 64 there.

Tennis began at The Homestead in 1892, and there now are 19 courts and a well-equipped tennis shop. A trap and skeet facility was built in the 1930's and the former home of the Fay Ingalls Memorial Skeet Shoot, named in memory of the resort's long-time president. From 1928 until 1966, an annual horse show drew entries from across the country. Riding is still important here with miles of bridle trails through the 16,000-acre estate. Non-equestrians may engage carriages to tour the area.

There are three swimming pools: an indoor pool at the Spa, a pool at the South Wing, and an outdoor pool with a sand beach. The Cascades Stream offers some of the best trout fishing in the Allegheny Mountains. Eight bowling lanes with automatic pin-setters are in the Spa. Two lawn-bowling courts are near the tennis courts. An outdoor playground for children is next to the Spa, with swings, slides, a merry-go-round, sandbox, wading pool, and tree house. For rainy days, there is an attended playroom where arts and crafts are taught.

Three riders start on a ride through the Allegheny mountains (above). Jigsaw puzzles are still in vogue here and this looks like a particularly difficult one (above right). The most envied swing in golf belongs to Homestead pro Sam Snead (right). Mr. Snead's favorite course is The Cascades (opposite). People were coming here for the healing springs and clear mountain air before the American Revolution.

The Homestead pioneered Southern skiing by building a million-dollar area with snow-making equipment, three trails, intermediate to expert, and five slopes, novice to expert, a double chair lift, a T-Bar and two rope tows. A well-equipped ski lodge is at the base at the 2,500-foot level. (The vertical drop of the ski area is 700 feet.) An Olympic-sized skating rink is next to the lodge, and skating and skiing lessons are available.

Changing times have put an end to one sport here: the traditional Homestead race in which waiters would navigate a course with a laden tray on their heads, guests betting heavily on their favorites.

The Spa is still a major attraction at The Homestead. The guests may use the Spa facilities casually, but for many a stay here involves a thorough examination by the attending physician and a

prescribed regimen. The core of the program is hydrotherapy. First, the patient stands in an enclosed bath with a spout of mineral water playing over his body, an adaption of Dr. Goode's technique. Then one luxuriates in a tub filled with the 104° water. A hot pack induces perspiration; finally, a cold shower tops off the treatment. The treatments vary from patient to patient, often including massage, a sauna, whirlpool baths, sun and infra-red lamps, and underwater exercises.

The food at The Homestead is justly famous, ranging from such regional favorites as Smithfield ham, hominy grits, and turnips and turnip greens "farmer style," to fine continental cuisine, expertly prepared and deftly served. The columned dining room is elegant, the menu extensive, and the music properly sedate. From April through October, one can dine in the Grille Room on such

specialties as tournedos Rossini, rack of lamb provençale, and roast fresh baby pheasant au madère with wild rice and grapes. A reasonable surcharge is added for this extravagance. A superb buffet is served daily in the Casino. Golfers may lunch at the restaurant in the Cascades Club. Picnic lunches also are available. A lovely tradition continues each afternoon at four-thirty when tea is served in the Great Hall to the accompaniment of a string ensemble.

Personages have been coming to The Homestead from the beginning. The old records detail a visit by Thomas Jefferson with an extra charge for the whiskey he consumed. During the 1930's, the queen of New York society, Mrs. Cornelius Vanderbilt, made her summer headquarters here. Other guests include: William Howard Taft, Woodrow Wilson, Warren G. Harding, Calvin Coolidge, Lyndon B. Johnson (all while they were in office), Franklin D. Roosevelt, Dwight D. Eisenhower, Richard Nixon, Nelson Rockefeller and Ronald Reagan. And still they come; during the summer season the guest list is a miniature "Who's Who."

After Pearl Harbor, the Japanese Diplomatic Corps were interned at The Homestead, and Italian and Vichy French diplomats at The Homestead's sister resort, The Cascades Inn. The diplomats were exchanged in 1942. In 1943, representatives of 44 nations met at The Homestead for the International Food Conference, a precursor of the United Nations.

The appeal of The Homestead goes beyond its incomparable setting and impressive facilities. In character, this is the most Southern of all the great resorts; it is aristocratic, charming and hospitable. Tradition at The Homestead weaves a spell that is enchanting.

THE

GREENBRIER

To Greenbrier guests the Spring House is the symbol of the gracious resort (overleaf). During the Civil War, the statue of Hygeia was shot off the roof. Action on the putting green is visible from a lounge window (opposite). This side-view of the hotel (right) was made from where the Old White once stood. After World War II, a redecorated Greenbrier reopened with an historic gala.

THE GREENBRIER

To experience this magnificent resort is to relive an interesting part of American history, for the Greenbrier is as old as the United States itself. Shawnee Indians revered the sulphurous "medicine waters" from the springs here and attributed great powers to them. In 1778, a young woman named Amanda Anderson, afflicted with crippling rheumatism, was seemingly cured after a period of drinking the water. The news quickly spread and Michael Bowyer, who owned the land around the springs, built a tavern and some guest cottages. Bowyer's son-in-law expanded the operation in the early 1800's, enlarging the tavern and building a row of cottages and two spring houses. A few years later, General Andrew Jackson paid a visit, fresh from his victory at New Orleans.

In the 1830's, the resort started to become fashionable. Cholera and yellow fever were rampant in the South, but White Sulphur Springs was spared. Soon wealthy planters were coming for extended stays, socializing and look for suitable marriage partners for their children. Henry Clay and John C. Calhoun were frequent visitors. During the financial panic of 1837, President Martin Van Buren and his advisors met at White Sulphur Springs to discuss rechartering the Bank of the United States. An English novelist, Frederick Marryat, was a guest that year and wrote, "I must say that I never was at any watering-place in England where the company was so good and so select as at the Virginia Springs in America."

The resort was taken over in 1857 by eight Virginia businessmen who built an impressive new hotel. It was 400 feet long and 100 feet wide, three stories high with a columned porch and a large dome—the largest building in the South. The dining room, the largest in the country could seat 1,200. It was named the Grand

Central Hotel but the name never took. It was "The White" and later "The Old White," and in its heyday it symbolized the aristocratic South.

The Civil War was understandably hard on the resort. It suspended operations after the 1861 season and suffered some damage from nearby battles. The statue of Hygeia was shot off the dome of the spring house. White Sulphur Springs also found itself in the new state of West Virginia. It reopened in 1867, uncertain what the future would bring. A race track was built and an artificial lake was created in an attempt to regain its pre-eminence.

What turned the trick, though, was a guest who arrived in 1867. General Robert E. Lee's wife, Mary, was badly crippled with arthritis, and he hoped the waters would bring some relief. The Lees brought their daughter Agnes, a maid and Mary Pendleton, a friend of Agnes. The Lees were the hit of the season. The general would chat with the men, and dance with the women. Many of his days were spent riding his horse "Traveller" in the nearby countryside. The Lees became regular guests. The following year, the general was joined by a number of his war time comrades, a reunion that resulted in the White Sulphur Manifesto: Lee and 31 other former Confederates affirmed loyalty to the Union and promised to treat the Negro fairly, asking that the South be treated fairly by the North and restored to self-government.

The Chesapeake & Ohio railroad reached White Sulphur Springs in 1869 and made it the only resort on the line that linked Baltimore and the Ohio River. This brought an influx of Northern visitors and extended the resort's social impact. The siding at White Sulphur Springs was used by the private railroad cars of the likes of J. Ogden Armour, William K. Vanderbilt, and various

41

Astors and Drexels. Elegant as it was, the resort was beset with financial problems which worsened as the 19th Century ended.

After three decades of dickering, the Chesapeake & Ohio took over in 1910. A new, 250-room Georgian-style hotel was completed in 1913 and named The Greenbrier. It was open year-round, the Old White only in the summer season. A nine-hole golf course opened in 1910; the 18-hole Old White course in 1914. Tennis courts were added and a golf and tennis club became the recreational center for the guests. New cottages were built. In all, the C & O invested more than two million dollars.

The investment paid off. White Sulphur Springs again was a playground for society. After World War I, the resort welcomed President Woodrow Wilson, General John J. Pershing, and David Windsor, the young Prince of Wales, who played golf and tennis, danced with a number of young ladies, and sat in with the dance band on drums. (As the Duke of Windsor, he returned several times in the late 1940's with the Duchess, who had honeymooned here with her first husband, Navy Lieutenant Earl Winfield Spencer.)

By the mid 1920's, the Old White had had its day. It was torn down and the Greenbrier expanded from 250 to 580 rooms. The cottages were restored or rebuilt, the golf courses redesigned, a private airport and polo field added. In 1936, Sam Snead, then 24, was hired as the golf professional. During his stay at The Greenbrier he was to win more major tournaments than any golfer in the world.

The Greenbrier made it through the Depression years only to find itself involved with World War II. After Pearl Harbor, it was used by the State Department to intern German diplomats. By the time the diplomatic prisoners were exchanged in July 1942, there were some 1,400 internees at The Greenbrier. Then the army

Tennis as the game was meant to be played draws a pair of onlookers (opposite). The Presidents' Cottage (above left) served as a Summer White House for Van Buren, Fillmore and Buchanan. John Tyler honeymooned here. A ride around the 6,500 acres in a carriage is a good way to see the sights (above). The leaves of autumn bring color to the gold course. A polo field was a 1920's hit.

purchased the hotel for use as a hospital. As Ashford General Hospital, it housed thousands of wounded combat veterans. The C & O repurchased The Greenbrier in 1946 for $3.5 million, the price the army had paid for it, and began a complete refurbishing program under the supervision of the interior designer Dorothy Draper.

The Greenbrier reopened in April 1948 with a grand ball. Among the guests were the Duke and Duchess of Windsor, Mr. and Mrs. John Jacob Astor, Mr. and Mrs. Anthony Biddle Duke, Perle Mesta, Elsa Maxwell, Bing Crosby, Fred Astaire, Louis B. Mayer and William Randolph Hearst, Jr. Social historian Cleveland Amory called it "the outstanding resort society function in modern social history."

Later guests were Prince Rainier and Princess Grace of Monaco, Prime Minister Nehru of India, and Presidents Johnson, Nixon and Carter. President Eisenhower came to The Greenbrier in 1956 to meet with the president of Mexico and the prime minister of Canada.

The Greenbrier is more glorious today than ever. Its 6,500 acres in an upland Allegheny valley are tended by 63 groundskeepers and gardeners, part of a total staff of 1,475—an employee for every guest. The hotel gleams, inside and out. Every guest room is decorated differently and beautifully, and is visited by a maid three times a day. The public rooms are splendid, closer in feeling to a great country house than a hotel. The paintings and *objets d'art* on display are worthy of a small museum. The rhododendron, state flower of West Virginia, is used in the hallway wallpaper pattern and on the dining room's flatware. Fresh flowers and flowering plants are everywhere. The formal gardens are beautiful from spring to late fall. The service at The Greenbrier once was

A holiday at The Greenbrier has been likened to visiting an English country estate (opposite). Even the indoor pool has a stately grandeur (upper left), as does the trio playing for high tea (far left). In the living room at the Presidents' Cottage, a mural above the fireplace and wainscotting shows how the resort looked in the early 1800's. General Robert E. Lee and his family summered here after the Civil War.

described as, "Ladies and gentlemen waiting on ladies and gentlemen." The description holds true today.

Guests may choose from more than 700 rooms and suites in the hotel. Families or small groups may prefer one of the 48 cottages. They are in rows—Paradise Row, Tansas, South Carolina, and Baltimore, the choice of Robert E. Lee—their porches forming continuous arcades. A delightful Greenbrier tradition is evening cocktails on the cottage porches. It was on a cottage porch that the then governor of South Carolina, James H. Hammond, said to the then governor of North Carolina, John Motley Morehead, "It's a long time between drinks." For the truly affluent there is the Valley View Estate House with four master bedrooms and a boardroom. The use of a limousine is included in the tariff.

Fine dining is part of the tradition at the Greenbrier. The main dining room is truly elegant; cut-glass chandeliers lighting the dark green walls hung with Colonial portraits, and gold-framed mirrors. An orchestra plays for dancing. Gourmets are attracted to the Tavern Room where many of the dishes are prepared at the table, for an additional charge on the resort's Modified American Plan. Dinner is also served at the Golf Club where a trio entertains. A stupendous buffet lunch is served here daily. There is a coffee shop for light snacks. Well-made drinks and good fellowship are to be found in the Old White Club and the Tavern Room Lounge. Both offer dancing after dinner.

The spa still is still an important part of The Greenbrier. There are saunas, steam rooms, whirlpools, scotch hoses, exercise rooms, an indoor pool and massage. If one has overindulged, there is the "Morning After Preservation"—a steam bath, a sauna, and an "Old White" massage—designed to make the night before just a pleasant memory.

Golfers will find the Lakeside (6,048 yards, par 70) relatively easy, and the Old White (6,600 yards, par 72) a sheer delight. Jack Nicklaus redesigned the Greenbrier course in 1979, in preparation for the Ryder Cup matches, and the 6,721 yard, par 72 course is a real test of golfing skill. On rainy days, golfers may repair to an indoor driving range. In addition there are 15 outdoor and five indoor tennis courts, platform tennis, an outdoor heated swimming pool, an eight-lane bowling alley, a skeet and trap club, horseback riding and surrey or sleigh rides, depending upon the season, badminton, horseshoes, hiking, jogging, a paracourse, and cross-country skiing.

A first-time visit to The Greenbrier should include the Presidents' Cottage Museum. Built in the early 1800's by a New Orleans sugar planter it later served as the Summer White House for Martin Van Buren, Millard Fillmore, and James Buchanan. John Tyler honeymooned in the cottage before becoming president. One first floor room is covered with murals of The Greenbrier in the early days; another is filled with Robert E. Lee memorabilia. Upstairs is a bedroom and sitting room with period furnishings. Also of interest is the Alabama Row Creative Arts Colony, home for a number of artists and crafts workers.

The Greenbrier is not simply the oldest and most historic of American resorts. By any yardstick, it is as fine a resort as there is in the world, and its blend of Southern hospitality and international sophistication is unique. To visit here is to savor the quintessence of the resort experience.

SEA PINES

PLANTATION

The sun says goodbye to Harbor Town (overleaf). A delightful pool beckons guests at the Hilton Head Inn (far left). Omelets are prepared to order in the Crow's Nest (near left). Boats tie up at the Harbor Town marina (below left). A small lake provides a natural setting for some Sea Pines homes (below right). Beachwalkers seem a light year from civilization (below). A golfer putts out near the landmark lighthouse (opposite).

SEA PINES PLANTATION

This semi-tropical island slumbered peacefully off the shore of South Carolina until the middle of the 20th Century. There had been a cotton plantation here, and the northern end had been fortified during the Civil War but only ruins remained of those enterprises. Yet ten years later, it had become the first planned resort community, a model of ecological planning and intelligent land development. It all came about because of the vision and drive of Charles Fraser, a young man fresh out of the Yale Law School.

Mr. Fraser's family was in the lumber business and had extensive holdings on the island. He was certain the island eventually would be developed, and he had seen examples of the evils of unrestricted commercial development up and down the East Coast. He vowed to develop it himself, retaining absolute aesthetic control. Over the years he did just that.

To visit Sea Pines Plantation today is to sense immediately the existence of a brilliant master plan. One is only vaguely aware of the hundreds of private homes and condominiums. Although mostly privately built, they all have uniform cedar-shake roofs and cypress siding, and they blend in with the environment. All are set back from the road, tucked in among the trees, mostly along the fairways of the three golf courses, or along the beachfront. No house seems to impinge on another. There are dozens of public walkways to the beach, and much money and effort has been spent to preserve the large trees intact. Today Sea Pines Plantation is about fully developed: more than 4,000 homes and villas, three golf courses, 80 tennis courts, two marinas, 25 public pools, three playgrounds, a 605-acre forest preserve, 41 miles of bicycle and jogging paths, 24 stables, 16 restaurants, and a first-class hotel, all on 4,500 acres. Yet the feeling everywhere is one of semi-wilderness.

Besides enlightened development, Charles Fraser showed the way to a new kind of resort. Instead of the traditional grand hotel, his is a resort of second homes and condominiums with shared recreational facilities. Vacationers can rent accommodations through the overseeing corporation during times designated by the individual owners. This concept, pioneered here, has fueled a 25-year boom in the American resort industry and changed the nature of resorts irrevocably. It is the rare resort now, even including the legendary ones, that is not in the condominium business in one way or another.

Guests may stay at the luxurious oceanfront Hilton Head Inn, or choose from an extensive range of accommodations: a house on a golf course or at the beach, an apartment or duplex at Harbour Town, with its famous lighthouse and a marina filled with as many spectacular craft as can be found anywhere, or at South Beach Village which looks as if it were transplanted intact from the New England coast. Wherever one stays, all the facilities are available, although an automobile is a must.

Sports are big time here. The Harbour Town Golf Links is the home of the Heritage Golf Classic, the Muscular Dystrophy Celebrity Pro-Am, the National Football League Super Bowl of Golf, and the Sea Pines Junior Heritage Golf Classic. Designed by Jack Nicklaus and Peter Dye, Harbour Town is rated by the *World Atlas of Golf* as one of the ten top courses in North America. Six of its holes were rated among the toughest 18 on the pro tour. Gary Player puts it even more strongly. He calls the 6,652-yard, par 71, course "the finest in the world." The 6,600-yard, par 72 Ocean Course, while less challenging, has a spectacular 15th hole that flirts with the Atlantic Ocean. The Ocean was designed by George Cobb and opened in 1960. Sea March is for the exclusive use of Sea Pines residents and their guests. Those in search of expert instruction will find it at the Bert Yancey Classic School of Golf, a system of instruction bases on the relaxed and graceful swings of the pre-World War II masters. Stan Smith is the tennis professional and there are tournaments throughout the year.

The restaurants at Sea Pines cater to every taste and budget, but gourmets head for the Audubon Room of the Inn to sample such specialities as oysters Audubon, baked oysters with shallots, tomato and fresh herbs, or a splendid bouillabaisse made with fresh local seafood, or fresh red snapper baked in a white wine sauce garnished with shrimps, scallops and crabmeat. On the top floor of the Inn is the Crow's Nest with an excellent bar, a commanding view, and a limited but tasty menu. An excellent choice is a stand where one—with the help of a cook, of course—can create an omellete to precise personal specifications.

If Sea Pines Plantation is truly the resort of the future, we may all relax: the future is in good hands.

49

PINEHURST

The front lawn at Pinehurst (overleaf) is as neatly trimmed as its fairways. The classic hotel, for years known as the Carolina, opened on New Year's Day 1901 with ten guests. Now it draws golfers from all over the world. The swimming pool (opposite) is a good place to loosen tight shoulder muscles. Besides the hotel, guests may stay in a variety of Pinehurst condominiums. The most unusual are these octagonal elevated cottages (left). Others are on a private lake.

PINEHURST

The bar at the main clubhouse at Pinehurst is aptly named the 81st Hole, for five courses fan out from this handsome building. Downstairs is a pro shop roughly the size of a shopping-mall department store, the headquarters of the teaching staff equipped to videotape one's swing for critical analysis, a computer that will handle tee-off reservations two months in advance, and enough golf carts to mobilize a small army. In a real sense, Pinehurst is the epicenter of the world of golf: it is almost impossible to enter a serious discussion of the game without dwelling on Pinehurst, its unmatched facilities and its long and glorious history. Yet, curiously, Pinehurst became a golf resort almost by accident.

James Walker Tufts, a Bostonian who had made his fortune in soda fountain equipment, wanted to build a health resort where Northerners could escape from the cold. He came to North Carolina in 1895 and was impressed with the climate and the nearby mineral springs. Tufts purchased 5,000 acres of sandy, ravaged timberland for one dollar an acre. He engaged Frederick Law Olmsted, the designer of New York City's Central Park, to build a replica of a New England village. Within six months, construction was completed on some 20 cottages, a boarding house, a general store, and the first hotel, the Holly Inn. During this period, Pinehurst was known as Tuftown. Tufts came across a list of entries in a contest to name a real-estate development, picked Pinehurst from it, and adopted it for his village and resort. More than 225,000 trees were planted on the acreage during the first two years. The Carolina Hotel, now the Pinehurst Hotel, was opened New Year's Day 1901 with ten guests. Three months later, it was filled to capacity.

Recreation was an important amenity at Pinehurst from the beginning. The two tennis courts built in 1896 for the guests at the Holly Inn were among the first in the country. Riding, polo, hunting, lawn bowling, bicycling, and archery were popular then

as now. But the early guests had found something else to amuse themselves. In 1898, an angry farmer approached Mr. Tufts and complained that guests were hitting little white balls into his pasture and frightening his cows. Dr. D. Leroy Culver of New York was retained to build a golf course, a rudimentary nine-hole affair that was completed in early 1898. In 1901, Mr. Tufts had the uncommon good fortune to hire a young Scottish golf professional to direct the golf operations at Pinehurst. He was Donald J. Ross and his first task was redesigning the No. 1 course, expanding it to 18 holes. Then he fashioned his masterpiece, the No. 2 course. No. 2 has been named one of the ten finest courses in the world—the favorite course of the immortal Sam Snead, among others. It was on No. 2 that a young Ben Hogan won his first major tournament. Donald Ross remained with Pinehurst until his death in 1948, designing Nos. 3, 4 and 5 as well. (No. 6 was built recently nearby, a 6,830-yard, par 72, designed by George and Tom Fazio.) During his career Ross designed or redesigned more than 400 golf courses throughout the North American continent.

By 1903, the Pinehurst Golf Club was established and playing host to the North and South Amateur Invitational. Through the years, the best in the world have played here—Harry Vardon, Bobby Jones, Gene Sarazen, Byron Nelson, Snead and Hogan, Arnold Palmer, Jack Nicklaus, Johnny Miller, Tom Watson, Glenna Collett Vare, Babe Zaharias, Patty Berg—all of them. It seemed only fitting that the World Golf Hall of Fame and its museum be established at Pinehurst. The impressive building forms a backdrop for the fourth green of No. 2 Course. President Gerald Ford dedicated the building in 1974. The interior is dominated by a larger-than-life full-length bronze statue of Bobby Jones, and the exhibits range from a wooden putter and a "play club" that were crafted by Scottish clubmaker Hendrie Millne of St. Andrews to an exhibit of clubs used by U.S. presidents. The curator of the

53

Clad in plus fours and knee socks,
a Pinehurst golf pro corrects
a neophyte's back swing (left).
A statue of the legendary
Bobby Jones (below) dominates the
interior of the World Golf Hall
of Fame next door to the resort.
Exhibits trace the history
of the game. Tennis clinics at
the club offer a quick way
to an improved game (below left).
Once trap and skeet were more
popular here than golf.
The reason: Annie Oakley and
her husband Frank Butler taught at
the range (below right).

54

At Pinehurst, Scottish influence is everywhere. Bellmen (left) wear traditional kilts and knee socks. An annual tournament sends winning guests to play golf on Scottish courses.

museum is Laurie Auchterlonie, who holds a lifetime appointment as honorary professional to the Royal & Ancient Golf Club at St. Andrews, Scotland.

Golf is taken very seriously indeed at Pinehurst but it would be a shame if this frightened away a beginner. In fact, there may be no better place to learn the game. There is year-round instruction by the staff—jauntily clad, it should be noted, in plus-fours and argyle golf socks—but the best arrangement for the beginner is to attend one of the five-day Golf Advantage Schools given from mid-March to late in October. One inclusive fee includes the works: five nights lodging, three meals a day, four days of instruction, daily greens fees and cart rentals, an opening cocktail party, and a closing tournament and banquet. School director Frank Palumbo and head professional Mike Sanders and their staff are the epitome of personalized intelligent instruction, and the difference four days can make in a beginner's game is amazing. In June and July, there are junior schools for youngsters 11 through 17.

The history of Pinehurst would not be complete without mention of the couple who ran the trap-and-skeet club here during the First World War—Frank Butler and his wife Annie Oakley. After 17 years starring in the Buffalo Bill Wild West Show, the Butlers moved to Pinehurst where Frank ran the club, and Annie taught and gave exhibitions. Annie's act starred Frank and their setter, Dave. She would shoot apples from Frank's and the dog's heads, and from the heads of the more adventurous guests. Annie also acted in theatrical productions at the hotel and took part in local minstrel shows, but her real forte was instruction. During her stay, she reportedly taught some 15,000 women to shoot, sometimes as many as 800 at a time, and the gun club rivalled the golf club in popularity. Each fall, the Pinehurst Gun Club hosts the Annie Oakley Trapshoot in her honor.

Tennis is somewhat overshadowed here which is not the fault of the Pinehurst Tennis Club. There are 24 courts, 18 clay and 6 all-weather, and the tennis clinics and junior camps run by former U.S. professional champion Welby Van Horn are as enjoyably productive as the Golf Advantage Schools. Nor is tennis here devoid of history: Bill Tilden won the first North and South Open at Pinehurst in 1919.

John Philip Sousa came to Pinehurst for the trapshooting. Bing Crosby for golf and hunting. Mary Pickford and Douglas Fairbanks simply to relax. Dr. Edward Everett Hale, author of "A Man Without a Country," was first pastor of the Village Chapel in Pinehurst. Kate Douglas Wiggin developed the idea for "Rebecca of Sunnybrook Farm" at Pinehurst. Edgar Guest, an active member of the golf club, wrote several poems about his game.

Famous or not, all guests are ministered to admirably at the hotel. The 310 guest rooms and 23 suites are commodious and comfortable; there also are some 200 golf club villas ranging in size up to three bedrooms. Dining on the American Plan is a joy. Particularly to be savored are such regional specialities as Chief Boles' original onion shortcake, fried chicken Maryland, and Roger's Pinehurst ice cream pie. Another highlight is a lethal drink called an "Ole Cliff"—a mixture of gin, vodka, Kahlua, and rum mixed with vanilla ice cream, an excellent poolside refresher.

One finds it hard to bogey a holiday at Pinehurst.

Mass production took away the names of golf clubs and gave them numbers. The old names keep cropping up, however, and it is helpful to know what they mean:

Play club	No. 1 wood
Brassie	No. 2 wood
Spoon	Nos. 3 & 4 wood
Driving iron	No. 1 iron
Mid-iron	No. 2 iron
Mid-mashie	No. 3 iron
Mashie iron	No. 4 iron
Mashie	No. 5 iron
Mashie niblick or spade mashie	No. 6 iron
Pitcher	No. 7 iron
Pitching niblick	No. 8 iron
Niblick or lofter	No. 9 iron

In an increasingly impersonal world, it is a pleasure to note that the putter has remained the putter.

55

THE CLOISTER

One look and you know The Cloister is aptly named (overleaf). This buffet lunch can tame the most voracious appetite (opposite). A fan window overlooks the lovely courtyard (far left). A covered bridge leads to the St. Simons Island Club (left). Guests have 72 holes of golf, 18 clay tennis courts, skeet and trap, horseback riding, three swimming pools, and five miles of beach at their disposal.

THE CLOISTER

Hard by the coast of Georgia are 12 golden isles, warmed by the Gulf Stream and cooled by off-shore breezes, covered with tall palm trees, pine and live oaks, redolent with history. Here are the ruins of James Oglethorpe's Fort Frederica. Here the oak timbers were cut for "Old Ironsides," the U.S.S. Constitution, and her sister ship, the Constellation. Here, reportedly, Blackbeard buried some of his pirate treasure. And here is grown the famous long-staple Sea Island cotton.

Howard Coffin, an automobile engineer who designed both the Hudson and the Essex, fell under the charm of the islands early in the century and bought 20,000 acres on Sapelo Island in 1910 for about $150,000. He ran a successful plantation there but dreamed of building an island resort. His chance came in 1926 when he bought all of Sea Island, 750 acres of high ground and 150 of marsh, for $24,277. He retained Schultz & Weaver, the architectural firm that had just designed The Breakers at Palm Beach, and plans were drawn up for a most impressive hotel. Mr. Coffin had second thoughts, however. He thought it would be better to start more modestly. He approached Addison Mizner, the architect who transformed Palm Beach into a showcase for millionaires and who had just completed his own hotel, The Cloister, at Boca Raton. Mr. Coffin wondered if Mr. Mizner might be interested in building him a "friendly little hotel." Mr. Mizner, whose real estate empire was crashing down around him, was most interested.

When the hotel was finished, it was a charming smaller version of Mr. Mizner's Cloister at Boca Raton. Sensing, perhaps, that he was about to lose Boca Raton, Mr. Mizner talked Mr. Coffin into naming the hotel The Cloister. It opened in October 1928 to a full house. A publicity genius, Charles F. Redden, was associated with the hotel and engineered the coup of having President Calvin Coolidge spend the 1928 Christmas holiday at The Cloister. President Coolidge was photographed planting a live oak and the picture was on front pages across the country.

The Cloister has attracted statesmen and celebrities ever since. President and Mrs. Herbert Hoover visited. So did Mayor Jimmy Walker of New York. Charles Lindbergh landed here on his way to Mexico after his solo flight to Paris. The Thomas E. Deweys licked their wounds here after his 1944 defeat. Mr. and Mrs. John D. Rockefeller, Jr. took a respite from the restoration of Williamsburg. Bobby Jones often played golf here and his 67 stood as a course record for 30 years. In 1931 Eugene O'Neill and his wife bought land from The Cloister and built a home on the beach; in his years on Sea Island he wrote "Ah Wilderness." Winston Churchill's daughter Sarah married Anthony Beauchamp at The Cloister in 1952. The same year, the hotel was host to Her Majesty Queen Juliana of the Netherlands and her consort, Prince Bernhard. Alben Barkley, "The Veep," honeymooned here. Jimmy

A lovely lady pays a backhand compliment (right). Until recently the course record here was held by Bobby Jones (far right). The beach coverings at The Cloister are distinctively shaped (below). The sand is extremely fine and hard packed.

Carter has been a frequent visitor.

Since 1940, it has been a tradition at The Cloister to photograph each of the couples honeymooning at the hotel, and the count now has passed 28,000. The photographs are in albums kept in an alcove off the lobby. Two honeymooners returning for their twenty-fifth anniversary were former Treasury Secretary William Simon and General William C. Westmoreland, who took a moment to look up their honeymoon pictures.

One measure of a great resort is the number of its guests who return, year after year. No resort rates higher in returnees than The Cloister. It attracts young Southern families in the summer, an older Northern crowd in the winter, and a regional mixture in the spring and fall. Guests are quite a homogeneous group: well-to-do, well-dressed, essentially conservative businessmen and professionals. The quiet beauty and impeccable service at The Cloister seem to be everything that they want. Doing what it does

so well helped The Cloister weather the Depression. In 1933, a year when many resorts were practically empty, The Cloister was full, turning away more than 1,000 reservations.

There is a wide range of accommodations available: the main hotel, the newer River House, the guest and beach houses, or a family might rent one of a number of attractive private houses near the hotel. All guests have three full-course meals daily as part of their American Plan rate. Besides the main dining room, guests may choose from the Patio, the Georgian and the South Georgian, lunch at the Beach Club or the golf clubhouse, take a light breakfast or high tea in the Solarium, and journey to Ocean Grove on Friday nights for a plantation supper. There is dancing nightly.

The Sea Island Golf Club, offering 54 holes of golf, is, curiously, not on Sea Island but on St. Simons, a few miles away from the hotel and linked by a small bridge. The clubhouse is reached by a half-mile drive lined by moss-draped live oaks. The ruins of

an 18th Century slave hospital can be seen nearby, and part of the clubhouse was once used as a corn storehouse for the plantation. Both were built of tabby, a native construction material made of oyster shells, sand, lime, and water.

Four challenging nines await the golfer: the 3,371-yard, par 36, Seaside; Marshside, 3,248 yards, par 36, which runs beside White Heron Lake; Plantation, 3,343 yards, par 36; and Retreat, 3,506 yards, par 36. Bobby Jones's record 67 was shot on the Seaside-Plantation combination. The Cloister also owns the St. Simons Island Club and its excellent 6,464, par-72 course. A long covered bridge leads to the clubhouse, an excellent example of plantation architecture.

The gardens surrounding the main hotel are a testament to good horticulture. Five miles of perfect beachfront run by The Cloister and its next-door colony of 300 private homes. The hard-packed beach is a swimmer's delight and there also are heated pools at the Beach Club and the hotel. Guests may avail themselves of horseback riding, the skeet and trap range, 18 clay tennis courts, fishing, boating and bicycling.

One should take time to see some of the interesting sights nearby—the ruins of Fort Frederica on St. Simons; Jekyll Island, now a state park, which was owned by a club of 100 of the richest men in the United States from 1887 until World War II, and Little St. Simons, 30 square miles of primitive beauty with dozens of species of wildlife. There is also a tour of the Sea Island Marshes conducted by the University of Georgia Marine Extension Service. The Cloister, of course, will handle all the details of one's excursions.

There are bigger resorts than The Cloister, and flashier ones, too, but none better. Its formula of quiet, gracious good taste and the lure of the golden isles is as potent now as it was some 50 years ago when the cream of Georgia society cheered its opening.

BOCA RATON

The Golden Age of Florida architecture lives in the statue of an houri (overleaf). Changing tastes are reflected in The Tower and The Cloister (left). Tower once was the tallest building in Florida. Lush landscaping was part of Addison Mizner's dream of creating the greatest resort in the world at Boca Raton.

BOCA RATON HOTEL AND CLUB

Addison Mizner went to Palm Beach in 1918 to die. The architect was 45, heavily in debt, and had lung and heart trouble. He got bored with dying, he would explain later, and found Palm Beach athirst for his style of architecture, once described as "Bastard-Spanish Moorish Romanesque Gothic Renaissance Bull-Market Damn-the-Expense Style." Soon he was the designer to High Society. A dowager once met him on the beach and took him to task for saying he didn't have time to design a home for her. "Here's your home," he said, sketching in the sand with a stick. She approved it, a draftsman quickly copied the sand sketch, and the home was built.

Mizner's dream was to build the greatest resort in the world at a practically uninhabited town 22 miles south of Palm Beach, called Boca Raton. He enlisted the aid of his brother, Wilson, a legendary raconteur and con-man, and Harry Reichenbach, a publicity genius, and formed the Mizner Development Corporation. The first advertisement of the corporation bore the headline, "I Am the Greatest Resort in the World. I Am Boca Raton, Fla." and in much smaller type, "A Few Years Hence." The advertisement concluded with the statement, "My future must be glorious. I have Addison Mizner to make it so."

In the first six weeks of land sales, the Mizners reputedly collected 26 million dollars. The Cloister Inn opened February 6, 1926, the most expensive 100-room hotel ever built. To reach the hotel, Mizner built El Camino Real, the widest road in the world, and in the middle was the "Grand Canal of Venice" complete with gondolas.

Among Mizner's investors were General T. Coleman duPont, Elizabeth Arden, Harold Vanderbilt, Jesse Livermore, Irving Berlin, Marie Dressler, George Whitney and Herbert Bayard Swope. It was the height of the Florida land boom, and the price of lots in Boca Raton jumped from several hundreds of dollars to more than $100,000. The Mizners played the boom for all it was worth, reinvesting their profits in choice lots. The bubble broke late in 1926, sales stopped and lawsuits started. The Mizners couldn't get out from under and they were through at Boca. The Cloister Inn closed.

Former Vice President Charles G. Dawes took over the Mizner Development Corporation and the Cloister Inn, selling the inn in 1928 to Clarence Geist, a colorful character who had made a fortune in utilities. Mr. Geist spent eight million dollars improving The Cloister and developing the surrounding acreage. He created the club in 1930. Members had to buy $5,000 worth of stock in the development company, pay dues of $100 a year, and meet the personal approval of Mr. Geist. Boca Raton flourished under his guiding hand, and was a premier resort when he died in 1938 at the age of 71. His will provided a $100,000-a-year underwriting of any operating deficit of The Cloister. Early in 1942, the Army took over The Cloister as a barracks for aviation cadets, and land west of Boca Raton was used as a bombing range. In 1944, hotel magnate J. Myer Schine bought the Boca Raton Hotel & Club for $3 million and after the war completely refurbished it.

Seeing Boca Raton today it is hard to realize that as late as 1950 it had a permanent population of less than 1,000. The great days were still ahead when, in 1956, Mr. Schine sold the resort to the immensely wealthy Arthur Vining Davis, chairman of the Board of Alcoa, who had already amassed large holdings in Florida. Mr. Davis' Florida properties were put into a new stock company, Arvida, and development of Boca Raton began. The Royal Palm Yacht and Country Club, a community of several hundred

The luxurious Beach Club is the latest addition to Boca Raton (opposite above). The Tower pool is a popular meeting place (opposite below left). Cloister dining room is properly posh (opposite below right). Seward Johnson Jr.'s statue *Cracking the Whip* adds a festive touch at the Beach Club. (right).

luxury homes, was built just south of the hotel. Then came University Park and Boca West. The town was growing rapidly. When Davis died in 1962, the Pennsylvania Railroad bought Arvida, continuing to finance further building in Boca Raton.

The hotel, however, was losing money. After some soul-searching, it was decided to turn the hotel into a year-round resort, and more than double its capacity by building a 25-story tower building. When it was nearly finished, the chairman of Arvida's board rode a construction elevator to the top. He was so impressed with the view he had another floor built to include a restaurant. For a short time, after its completion in 1969, the tower was the tallest building in Florida. On the Tower's 25th floor is the palatial Presidential Suite, a four-bedroom complex that rents for $1,500 a day in season. (It's almost always rented.)

The third face of luxury at Boca Raton is, for all practical purposes, a new hotel complete unto itself: the Boca Beach Club, a 212-room futuristic seven-story beauty which is as posh as any hotel anywhere. When one arrives at the two-year-old Beach Club there is a welcoming glass of champagne. A personalized credit card is prepared so that there is no need for cash during the stay. Most rooms have balconies overlooking the white beach in front of the hotel. There are 28 tennis courts, sauna, whirlpool, a mini-gym, and a parcours. The Gulf Stream comes closest to Florida

at Boca, and as a result the deep-sea fishing is superb.

There are eight dining areas for the pleasure of the guests, and three certainly should be visited. The baronial main dining room in The Cloister, the Top of the Tower with the panoramic view up and down the coast, and the Shell Dining Room at the Beach Club, the plushest of them all. The chef is particularly adept with the fresh local fish—pompano, red snapper, grouper, and, of course, shrimp.

There is an 18-hole golf course at Boca, designed in 1928 by Red Lawrence and re-designed in 1959 by Robert Trent Jones. The 6,695-yard, par 71, course is quite flat but the narrow fairways can be troublesome. Guests also may play any of the four courses at Boca West, which is affiliated with the hotel. The club house is particularly attractive and a good choice for a light lunch.

Connoisseurs of resorts find Boca Raton fascinating. The Cloister, the Tower, the golf villas and the Beach Club are imaginative approaches to luxury and all say a lot about the fashion of the times in which they were built. To see them coexisting as functioning parts of the same resort is a short course in resort planning. There is a beautifully restored power boat, circa the 1920s, agleam with varnished wood and polished brass to take guests from The Cloister and the Tower to the Beach Club and back. It is most aptly named. Gold letters announce that it is "Mizner's Dream." 67

THE BREAKERS

In the dining room (overleaf), a massive chandelier hangs from the domed ceiling. The Doge's Palace in Venice inspired the ceiling and wall paintings in the Gold Room (left). Real breakers pound the seawall outside (opposite above) while golfers take the measure of the classic course outside.

THE BREAKERS

Ponce de Leon discovered Florida in 1513, Henry M. Flagler some 350 years later, but the effect on the state was every bit as great. A partner of John D. Rockefeller and a co-founder of Standard Oil, he was 55 and one of the richest men in the country when his doctor recommended that he go to Florida for his health. At that time, the railroad only went as far south as Jacksonville, a city of 15,000 people, the largest community in the state. Mr. Flagler, who despised cold weather, liked the climate. He and his second wife honeymooned at St. Augustine in 1884. While they were there a cold wave struck most of the country, but St. Augustine remained warm and sunny. Mr. Flagler now became a man with a mission.

A few months later, he purchased land in St. Augustine and commissioned the building of a grand hotel, the Ponce de Leon. He later built two more Spanish style hotels there, the Alcazar and the Casa Monica. A reporter for *Harper's Weekly* likened them to Aladdin's palaces. By now, Mr. Flagler had acquired the Florida East Coast Railway and the state offered him handsome incentives to extend the line further south. Nearly 250 miles south of St. Augustine, the tracks reached the shores of Lake Worth. Across the lake was a 14-mile spit of land with a few small houses on it called Palm Beach. A shipwreck offshore had spilled coconuts, and palms covered most of the land.

Mr. Flagler began to develop the area. He laid out a town on the mainland side called West Palm Beach, and on Palm Beach he built one of the largest resort hotels in the world, the six-story, wooden, 540-room Royal Poinciana. He then built a second hotel at the ocean. It was wooden like the Royal Poinciana, smaller but equally elegant. It was named the Palm Beach Inn, but the name was soon changed to The Breakers. A golf course and a park separated the two hotels, and guests could go from one to the other in miniature railroad cars pulled by donkeys. Mr. Flagler seemed content with his accomplishments and had no plans to extend his railroad farther south. A change in the weather and an odd gift changed his mind.

A severe cold wave hit north Florida in 1894, ruining most of the citrus crop. Freight shipments of orange crates on the railroad fell from 5,500,000 to 150,000. Shortly after, a railroad executive was in Miami, then nothing more than a small village. He met a widow, Mrs. Julia Tuttle, who believed Miami could prosper if the railroad came. She gave the executive a box of fresh orange blossoms, proof that the freeze hadn't touched south Florida. "Take them to Mr. Flagler," she said. Soon Mr. Flagler's railroad was laying track to Miami, and he had agreed to build a terminal, a municipal water system, and streets. He also acquired land on Biscayne Bay and built the first luxury hotel there, the Royal Palm, which opened in January 1897. Miami was soon flourishing, but Mr. Flagler felt more at home in Palm Beach. The old money was discovering Palm Beach and many were building second homes there.

Mrs. Flagler had been troubled with mental illness for some time and was permanently confined to an institution in 1896. The couple was divorced in 1901 and a week later the 71-year-old multimillionaire took 34-year-old Mary Lily Kenan as his third wife, a scandal of major proportions at the time. The new Mrs. Flagler wanted a mansion in Palm Beach and she got it, Whitehall, described in the *New York Herald* as "grander and more magnificent than any other private dwelling in the world." Conservative estimates put the cost at $2,500,000.

And it was his new wife who convinced him to extend his railroad all the way to Key West, an engineering feat that took seven years to complete. Mr. Flagler died at the age of 84, 14 months after the railroad was completed.

A royal palace would be proud of this ceiling in The Breakers (left). A poolside display of creative cuisine replete with an ice carving (opposite above) One young miss isn't intimidated by the ornateness around her (opposite below left). A thirst-quenching array of liquid refreshment comes with a winning smile (opposite below right). Once the rich arrived here by train for the season, now it is a year-round resort attracting the merely affluent year-round, from the four corners of the globe.

On March 18, 1925, a small fire broke out in a bedroom at The Breakers and spread rapidly. The water pressure was insufficient to contain the fire and the hotel burned to the ground. The company decided to rebuild The Breakers, a project that was completed at the end of 1926. Architect Leonard Schultze designed a seven-story, twin-towered structure with more than 500 guest rooms. The hotel interior, then and now, is grander than any other in America. The grand lobby has frescos on its vaulted ceilings. The Doge's Palace in Venice inspired the ceiling of the Gold Room, the Palace Davanzate in Florence was the model for the carved and inlaid ceiling in the domed dining room. From the day it opened, The Breakers was the most opulent resort anywhere.

The Breakers is the only Flagler hotel still in operation. Fearing another fire, the company ordered the wooden Royal Poinciana torn down a few years after The Breakers opened. The Ponce de Leon in St. Augustine is now Flagler College. The Alcazar is used to house city offices. Others have been torn down to make room for modern buildings. Whitehall now is the Henry Morrison Flagler Museum. But The Breakers by itself is quite sufficient to recall the Golden Age of Palm Beach and Florida hotels. It set a standard of luxury that has been unchallenged to this day.

Dining at The Breakers is as lavish as the setting. At breakfast there's a smartly turned out buffet with fresh fruit juices, hot and cold cereals, scrambled eggs, eggs Benedict, bacon, ham, sausage, and various specialties of the day. The evening repast is a sumptuous affair, continental cuisine expertly prepared and beautifully served. An orchestra plays for dancing. The wine list is more of a wine book, for the cellar contains more than 100,000 bottles of some 400 different vintages. Breakfast and dinner are included in the room rates; lunchtime finds most guests at either the Beach Club or the Golf Club. The lobby is the setting for the four o'clock tea during the season. After dinner, the Alcazar Lounge is a favorite watering hole.

For most if its life, The Breakers was open only for the three-month winter season. Now it's open year round with substantially lower off-season rates. There are 567 rooms and suites with either an ocean or garden view. A staff of 1,200 keeps the resort running smoothly.

The old Ocean golf course, 6,008 yards, par 70, is more charming than challenging. Guests may also use the newer 7,101-yard, par 71, Breakers West Course in West Palm Beach. Water hazards lurk on 14 of its holes and its contoured greens require precision putting. The hotel owns a mile of beach frontage, and there is an outdoor salt-water pool. There are nine Har-Tru and five Plexipave tennis courts, a clubhouse and a fine teaching staff of pros. Other recreational activities include croquet, lawn bowling, shuffleboard, and bicycling. The more sedentary are offered bridge, backgammon and dance lessons.

A trip to The Breakers should include a walk down Worth Avenue to see the array of super deluxe shops and galleries, and a drive to view the magnificent homes. Palm Beach is a true bastion of old money and the good life that it can buy. It is a perfect setting for a jewel of a resort, The Breakers.

73

INNISBROOK

Condominiums peek through the palm trees (overleaf).

A guest is always only a few steps away from golf (left) Heavy hitters practice their drives before a tournament (opposite above). A hearty lunch awaits guests enjoying a sail on Tampa Bay (opposite below left) One look tells why Gulf shrimp is world-famous (opposite below center). The joys of the 19th hole.

INNISBROOK

Most golf courses in Florida come equipped with bulldozed hummocks, sprawling scalloped sand traps, and lots of little water hazards—artifices designed to disguise the billiard-table flatness of the land. Then how does one account for Innisbrook? Its 1,000 acres just west of the Tampa Bay area are rolling and wooded, brightened by azaleas, hibiscus, and citrus groves, and dotted with real lakes.

The setting lends itself to 63 holes of high-caliber golf. The 27-hole Copperhead course meanders through cypresses, live oaks, and tricky water hazards, and has more dog-legs than the average kennel. Par is 71 and plays between 6,800 and 7,000, depending upon the 18 chosen. Equally formidable is the Island course, 6,999 yards, par 71. Both have been named among the top 100 courses in the country by *Golf Digest*. The shortest course is the Sandpiper, 6,087 yards, par 70, but if long drives aren't necessary accuracy is. The 600 acres of lakes and streams, well-placed traps and tree-lined fairways present a challenge unique in Florida. (The three courses have a total of 33 water hazards.) Each course has its own handsome clubhouse, complete with pro shop, lounge and dining room.

Innisbrook is a masterpiece of planning and design. It is a large resort that feels intimate. There are 1,223 guest suites in 25 attractive two-story lodges. All the rooms have private patios or balconies, color television, and kitchenettes. The lodges cluster around the golf courses and there is a swimming pool for every five lodges. Jitneys appear at a moment's notice to whisk guests from one center of activity to another, including several excellent Gulf Shore beaches. There are 11 Har-Tru and seven Laykold tennis courts, six indoor requetball courts, miniature golf, jogging trails, health club, basketball, horseshoes, and excellent fresh-water and deep sea fishing can easily be arranged. There is a supervised activities program for youngsters. Innisbrook is partial to athletic youngsters: several junior golf tournaments are held here each year, and an annual international junior women's tennis tournament, named in honor of Maureen Connolly, draws entrants from more than 40 countries.

Many Florida seafood restaurants advertise "fresh fish" and serve frozen red snapper from Korea. At Innisbrook, fresh means caught that day and nothing else. The best place to enjoy the harvest of the sea is at the posh Regency Room in the Island Clubhouse. Among the delights are shrimp Madras, with coconut and chutney, salmon Troisgros, scallops and snow peas, seafood Venetian, grouper en papilote, and crabmeat imperial. Oysters Beinville make a tasty appetizer, Greek bread a nice accompaniment, and for a finale, a Linzer torte or an English sherry trifle. If one is still mobile there is dancing to a trio at the Island Clubhouse or a choice of two musical reviews at the Copperhead nightclub. For the weary, a fleet of former post office delivery carts speed room service on its way.

Innisbrook is a half-hour from the Tampa International Airport and convenient to all of the attractions of Central Florida—Disney World, Busch Gardens, Weeki Wachee and Sea World, among others. In the town of Tarpon Springs is the community of Greek fishermen who dive from their picturesque boats for the sponges that made Tarpon Springs famous.

THE DORALS

Championship golf is all around her but this young guest seems to have other things on her mind (overleaf). A glittering array of ceiling lights greets diners at the Doral Hotel-on-the-Ocean (opposite above). The sleek hotel forms an impressive part of the Miami Beach skyline (opposite below left). And what is a resort without a beautiful girl (opposite below right), basking in the sun? A formal pool (left) is part of the handsome landscaping at the Doral Country Club. This golf complex is only minutes away from the Miami airport.

THE DORALS

The emergence of Miami as a city began when Henry M. Flagler's railroad reached it in 1896. The emergence of Miami Beach as a resort began when Carl Fisher, a rich Hoosier who had built the Indianapolis Speedway, financed a bridge to the island. He cleared the mangrove swamps, and soon the great Florida land boom was on. At its height, Fisher was entertaining Will Rogers, Jack Dempsey and Warren G. Harding in Miami Beach, by then an incorporated city with hotels, a polo field, a golf course, and tennis courts. The boom collapsed in 1925 and the Great Hurricane of 1926 dealt Miami Beach a second blow.

Many middle-class tourists visited Miami Beach during the Depression, helping the hotels to stay open. In World War II, practically all of the hotels were used to house Army Air Corps cadets, many of whom returned later and became permanent residents. After the war, Miami Beach enjoyed a building boom that lasted more than 20 years.

The Doral Hotel-on-the-Ocean was finished in 1963 at a cost of $22 million, the last and most luxurious of the beach hotels. From a broad, two-story base, it rises in a gray-green glass tower to a height of 17 floors. At the top is the Doral Roof Garden, as fine a gourmet restaurant as there is on Miami Beach, and the Starlight Roof Supper Club where thousands of tiny lights twinkle in the ceiling. The 430-room hotel is beautifully furnished with antiques, hand-woven rugs, hand-carved furniture, and hand-loomed tapestries. Opulence is everywhere. The Doral was Richard M. Nixon's headquarters at the 1968 Republican Convention.

The beach, recently enlarged by the Army Corps of Engineers to a width of 90 yards, is at TheDoral's doorstep. An expansive two-story cabana club rings an Olympic-sized pool. Private docking facilities are available directly across from the hotel's entrance on Indian Creek. There is a "Spa in the Sky" on the 16th floor, and a profusion of lobby shops, restaurants and lounges.

The second Doral is the Doral Country Club, a 2,400-acre resort near the Miami International Airport. Like the ocean hotel, it was built by Alfred L. Kaskel. (Doral is an acronym derived from Al and his wife's name, Doris.) The land originally was a swamp but today it is as lovely as anything in south Florida. The center of activity is the Clubhouse. Lodges nearby provide 660 extraordinarily comfortable guest rooms.

There are four 18-hole championship courses, and a par-3 executive course with full-sized greens. In addition there are 19 tennis courts, a swimming pool, baseball diamond, basketball courts and other facilities, including lakes stocked for fishing.

The five golf courses are designated by color, the most famous being the Blue (commonly called the "Blue Monster"), a 7,065-yard, par 72, endurance test with 114 traps and 22 lakes. The Doral Eastern Open is played here each year, and the pros have voted the 18th hole the hardest par 4 on the tour. The Gold, designed by Bob Von Hagge and Bruce Devlin is 6,480 yards, par 71, and winds around 17 lakes. The White, also designed by Mr. Von Hagge, is 6,726 yards, par 72, has 12 lakes and 92 bunkers. Reputedly the easiest course is the Red, 6,480 yards, par 71, designed by Dick Wilson. A nine-hole course is called The Green.

All the amenities, golfing and otherwise, are here. A delightful place to have dinner is on the large covered terrace overlooking the courses and a fountain in a nearby lake. The fresh stone crabs with mustard sauce and drawn butter, veal Oscar, and the yellowtail meunière are especially recommended.

The nicest part about TheDorals is that one doesn't have to choose between them. Guests at either Doral have the full use of the facilities of both Dorals, and there is regular limousine service between them. All in all, a lovely way to enjoy the best of both Miamis.

GRAND HOTEL
Point Clear

GRAND HOTEL

POINT CLEAR, ALABAMA

Point Clear juts far out from the eastern shore of Mobile Bay, its miles of sandy beaches catching the cooling southwest winds of spring and summer. The first hotel was built in this idyllic spot in 1847 with lumber brought over by boat from Mobile. It was a two-story, rambling building about 100 feet in length. It contained some 40 guest rooms, with other facilities housed in separate structures. The bar was called "Texas," because it was so far from the hotel. There were two wharves, one for men and one for women, as mixed bathing just wasn't done in those days.

During the Civil War much of the hotel was used as a hospital to treat the Confederate wounded from the Siege of Vicksburg. In the last year of the war, the 21st Alabama Regiment camped on the grounds. The hotel resumed operations after the war but on the night of July 4, 1869, a fire began in the kitchen and, fanned by high winds, destroyed the kitchen and the main hotel. The 150 guests escaped with their belongings. Lost in the fire were the records of the more than 300 soldiers who had died here at the hospital and were buried in a plot near what is now the ninth green of the golf course. The hotel continued operation with the undamaged buildings. A few years later, the 27-ton steamer Ocean Wave blew up as it prepared to leave the Point Clear Pier, killing more than 20 of its passengers and injuring many more. The Texas bar was used as an emergency hospital.

In 1875, Captain H. C. Baldwin, a well-known steamship captain, and his son-in-law, George Johnson, treasurer of Louisiana, built a new hotel, the first to be called the Grand Hotel. After the new 60-room hotel was completed, it became the center of social life in the area. By the turn of the century it was known as the "Queen of Southern Resorts." An 1893 hurricane demolished the dining room and the Texas bar, but the resort was soon back in full swing. In 1940, the old hotel was demolished and the present hotel built. Heartpine flooring and framing from the old hotel

was used. It was closed for most of World War II except for a nine-month period when it was a Marine training school. The Marines took their shoes off before entering the main building to protect the beautiful wooden floors.

The Grand Hotel today is a low-slung building with two residential wings fanning out from the lobby. There are 50 more guest rooms in the nearby Bay House, and several brick duplex cottages. In the dining room overlooking the bay, there is soft music while the guests enjoy such regional specialities as red snapper, giant shrimp and crayfish. There are three courses with 27 holes of golf: the Magnolia, designed by Joe Lee (3,248 yards), the Azalea (3,292 yards) and the Dogwood (3,421), both designed by Perry Maxwell. All are par 36 and are served by the Lakewood Golf Club. Grassy rolling fairways dog-leg through tall pines and live oaks. There is an alligator or two in the lagoons. The resort's 500 acres include a stunning, 750,000 gallon freshwater swimming pool 150 feet in diameter, 10 Rubico tennis courts, a yacht basin where one can rent a Rhodes 19 sailboat or go deep-sea fishing on the Billfisher, a 53-foot Hatteras sports fisherman. Less ambitious anglers can fish off the hotel's pier.

Lucky summer guests may experience a phenomenon unique to Mobile Bay in the Western Hemisphere. Without warning, fish of every description come out of the bay and cover a stretch of beach. The phenomenon lasts for several hours. Lookouts are posted around the bay and beat pots and pans when the fish are spotted. Everyone then comes to reap a free harvest from the sea, and a celebration begins—an Alabama Jubilee.

Two other treats are more predictable. From Julep Point, the sunsets are theatrically beautiful. And what better accompaniment at Julep Point could there be than a mint julep fashioned by Bucky? He's been making them here for nearly four decades, with mint picked fresh from his own garden outside the bar.

Miss Mescalero in tribal costume poses with the inn and Sierra Blanca in the background (overleaf). Skiers carve their way down the steep slope at the Sierra Blanca ski area (opposite). Like the inn, the area is owned and operated by the tribe. The modern inn (left) faces the snow-capped mountain. The Mescalero have held the mountain sacred for centuries. This rugged terrain offers some of the finest big game hunting in the Southwest.

INN OF THE MOUNTAIN GODS

MESCALERO, NEW MEXICO

The Apaches were a hard people in a hard land. They were hunters, not farmers like the Hopis. They lived in tepees, not villages like the Pueblos. They suffered greatly at the hands of the white man and when they went on the warpath, "Apache!" became the most frightening word in the Territory of New Mexico. Consider Nana, an old and sickly chief who led 40 Apache braves on a two-month, thousand-mile rampage in 1881. They killed 40 whites, wounded nearly 100, won eight pitched battles, captured 200 horses, eluded 1,400 troops and armed civilians finally escaping to a Mexican hideaway without losing a man.

Sierra Blanca is sacred to the Apaches. They find spiritual inspiration in the snow-capped peak. The mountain now is part of the Mescalero Apache Indian Reservation, some 450,000 acres of beautiful mountains and forests. Skiing came to this 12,003-foot mountain in the early 1960's under the leadership of Tribal President Wendell Chino. Now there is a four-passenger gondola and

six chair lifts with a capacity of 9,250 skiers an hour, snow-making equipment, and 25 runs on the 2,100-foot drop. Forty percent of the runs are rated beginner, 40 percent intermediate, and the rest expert. An attractive lodge and restaurant is at the base. This is where West Texas comes to ski. The standard joke on the slopes is to ask a newcomer, "What part of Texas are you from?"

The next tribal project was to build the Inn of the Mountain Gods, a brilliant modern building with a wall of glass looking out on Lake Mescalero and Sierra Blanca in the distance. The other three sides of the main building are all roof. The inn's 250 guest rooms are in lodges connected to the inn by enclosed passageways. In the lobby is a three-story, copper-sheathed fireplace. Off the lobby is a shop managed by Mrs. Chino that has as fine a collection of Indian jewelry and art as can be found in the Southwest. Throughout the inn are excellent examples of Indian arts and crafts, most of them personally selected by Mrs. Chino. Trophies

89

White Buffalo, a Comanche craftsman, fashioned the head of a chief from gold and silver (right). A magnificent spider-web turquoise is set in a gold bracelet with ring to match (below) by Navaho artisan Gibson Nez. Indian jewelry of superb quality is on sale at the inn.

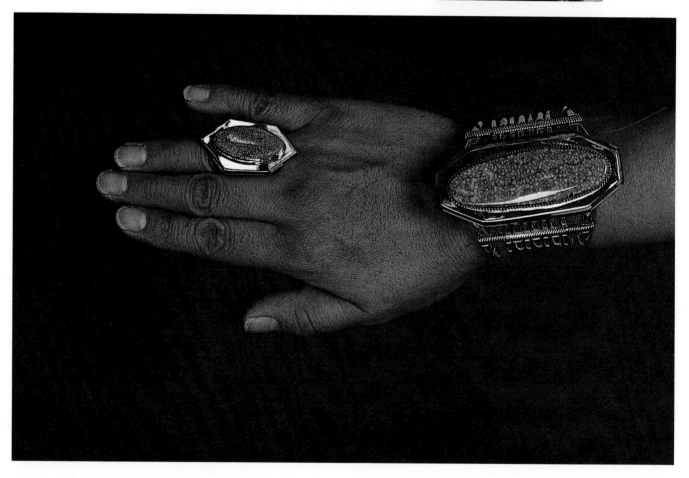

of bear, antelope, elk and mountain lion attest to the quality of hunting on the reservation. Many sportsmen use the inn as their base for expeditions into the mountains. The Dan-Li-Ka Room has cuisine worthy of any first-class resort. Fresh trout from Lake Mescalero is particularly recommended. There is a piano bar in the lobby where Teddi Sullivan performs vintage standards in a husky voice. Upstairs the Ina-da Lounge presents night club revues and dancing.

An 18-hole golf course was opened in 1976, a 6,819-yard, par 72 excursion around the west end of the lake. The 10th hole is unusual: one hits to an island then over the water again to the green. The clubhouse Apache Tee bar is a good spot to rehash one's game. There are six outdoor tennis courts and two in a bubble, all Laykold, a tennis clubhouse and excellent teaching facilities. Saddle horses, pack trips and trail rides are available through the stable. The 130-acre lake is generously stocked with trout. Sailing

and canoeing can be arranged. Blessedly, no power boats are allowed on the lake.

In nearby Alamogordo is the International Space Hall of Fame, and 15 miles southwest of the city is the White Sands National Monument, stretches of snow-white dunes of gypsum sand. At the White Sands Missile Range is the Trinity Project, now a National Historical Monument, where the first atomic bomb was exploded. It created a crater, 400 yards wide and eight feet deep, and its heat fused sand into a glasslike green solid. A few miles from the inn is the town of Ruidoso, home of Ruidoso Downs Racetrack where quarterhorses race from May to September. Here on Labor Day is run the All-American Futurity, the richest horserace in the world with a purse of $2,500,000.

To see what Apache life once was, one should visit the inn in the first week of July. The devil dance and the dance to celebrate the puberty rites of tribal maidens are unforgettable.

Aspens weather the winter on the slopes of Sierra Blanca (below). A gold and silver concho belt (bottom left) is inset with Love Mountain turquoises. Lee A. Yazzie, a Navaho master craftsman placed diamonds in the buckle. Another Gibson Nez piece (bottom right) has Nevada Blue turquoises in the pendant and matching ring.

BROADMOOR

The Broadmoor seems to be winking as twilight falls (overleaf). Painted ceilings and an elaborate chandelier set a formal mood (opposite). Silver bowl and tray are part of the art collection amassed by Mrs. Penrose. A cherub on the wall (left) sees all but tells no secrets. The Broadmoor reflects the personal tastes of the Penroses.

THE BROADMOOR

In a way, Colorado Springs was a resort from the beginning. Its dry mountain air could arrest and sometimes cure consumption, as tuberculosis was called a century ago. The town was founded in 1871 by William Jackson Palmer, a Civil War hero and railroad promoter, and soon healthseekers began to settle at the base of the Rockies. A Prussian count named James Pourtales came and bought a half interest in a dairy farm called Broadmoor at the foot of Cheyenne Mountain. He dammed a stream to create a small lake, talked the town into extending the street car tracks to his property, borrowed $400,000, and built a casino. It opened in 1891 and soon was a success, offering boating on the lake, the best food in town, and liquor—something not available in dry Colorado Springs. The count soon was planning a grand hotel but something happened. Gold was discovered at Cripple Creek 18 miles away.

Count Pourtales contracted a severe case of gold fever. He invested $80,000 in a Cripple Creek claim. Although the Cripple Creek gold field became the richest in the United States and the count's holdings increased in value to three million dollars, he managed to overextend himself and lose everything, including the casino. The casino burned down in 1897, and the new owners built a smaller casino to take its place. The count was able to recoup some of his fortune in Arizona and eventually retired to Europe in comfort.

Two Philadelphians fared much better at Cripple Creek, Spencer Penrose and his partner Charles L. Tutt, Jr. Mr. Penrose, who traced his ancestry back to an associate of William Penn's, was the youngest of six brothers. The other five distinguished themselves at Harvard, while Penrose barely managed to graduate. What he lacked in scholarship, however, he made up in business acumen. With his inheritance, he and his partner bankrolled Cripple Creek prospectors and reaped immense profits. They duplicated their success in the Utah copper mines. By 1910, Spencer was the largest stockholder in the Kennecott Copper Corporation, a multimillionaire with a tax-free income in excess of $200,000 a year. He retired and spent his time touring the world with his wife. The Penroses were demanding guests at the great hotels of Europe, and Mr. Penrose began to dream of building his own resort and running it the way he thought a resort should be run.

Returning to Colorado Springs, he scouted around for a suitable property. He wanted to buy The Antlers Hotel but negotiations were unsuccessful. Keeping busy with civic projects, Mr. Penrose was instrumental in building the road to the top of Pike's Peak, and, in 1915, celebrated the accomplishment by inaugurating the Pike's Peak Hill Climb—the hell-for-leather automobile race up the steep slope. The next year he made an offer for the Broadmoor property; the owners accepted and he started planning his resort.

The casino was moved and converted into a golf clubhouse. To build his hotel, Mr. Penrose retained the architectural firm of Warren & Wetmore, designers of New York's Grand Central Station. Frederick Law Olmsted, who created New York's Central Park, was to be the landscape architect. The nine-story hotel was built facing Cheyenne Mountain on the eastern side of the lake. Its style was Mediterranean with pink stucco walls. The interiors were a pleasing mixture of period decorating, reflecting what had impressed the Penroses most in their world travels. Mr. Penrose wanted to retain the name Broadmoor for his resort but found that it now was in the public domain. To get around this, the name was spelled with a small raised capital "A"—BRO^ADMOOR—a trade mark still in use today.

The Broadmoor opened on June 29, 1918, with a formal dance for more than 200 guests. From the beginning, it was popular with the rich and famous, many of whom were personal friends of the Penroses. The King of Siam and the Archduke of Austria were early visitors. Later arrivals included Jack Dempsey and Shirley Temple. Herbert Hoover was welcomed, but when

95

Franklin D. Roosevelt, then the 1932 Democratic presidential candidate, came, Mr. Penrose arranged to be out of town.

The Penroses made the Broadmoor their lives, sparing no effort or expense to make it better and more beautiful. Two more golf courses were added, two outdoor swimming pools, a race track and a stadium (since gone), a zoo, a chapel, and an ice arena that twice has been the site of the World Figure Skating Championships. Mrs. Penrose decorated the public spaces with her museum-quality collection of Oriental antiques and important European and American paintings. In the 1920's, Mr. Penrose commissioned Maxfield Parrish to paint the resort. In the painting, which now hangs in a sitting room in the hotel, Mr. Parrish has moved the hotel to the other side of the lake to heighten the effect of lake, hotel and mountain. Shortly before Mr. Penrose's death in 1939, he built on the side of Cheyenne Mountain a tower and carillon in memory of his friend, humorist Will Rogers.

Today the Broadmoor has lost none of its elegance and charm. Two new guest buildings have been added: Broadmoor South, on the lake next to the original hotel, and Broadmoor West, across the lake. Atop Broadmoor South is the excellent Penrose Room, with Edwardian decor, continental food, and a dazzling night view of the lights of Colorado Springs. In Broadmoor West is Charles Court, a gourmet restaurant of national repute, decorated in the style of an English country manor. In the original hotel the guest will find the majestic main dining room, the tropical Garden Room, and the Tavern, decorated with original Toulouse-Lautrec lithographs.

Mr. Penrose was an oenophile, and glass cases around the Tavern contain some of the highlights of his collection: Lafite Rothschilds, Chateau Margaux, and La Tours dating from the 1860's, displayed next to brandy from the private cellar of Chester A. Arthur. On the eve of Prohibition, Mr. Penrose had eight rail-

The sunny Garden Room at the Broadmoor (opposite) looks out across the lake to the Rockies beyond. The Charles Court at Broadmoor West offers gourmet dining and a view of the hotel (left). A bust of the late humorist Will Rogers, a friend of the resort's founder, stands in front of the tower and carillon built in his honor (below). At night, the hotel looms against the lights of Colorado Springs.

road cars of liquor delivered to the cellars of the Broadmoor. It was illegal to sell it to his guests, but he and his friends weathered Prohibition in grand style.

The current excellence of the Broadmoor is due to the stewardship of two descendents of Mr. Penrose's partner: Thayer Tutt, chairman emeritus, and his brother, Russell Tutt, chairman and chief executive officer.

The recreational facilities match the hotel in quality. Donald Ross, the first great golf architect, designed the original course, Broadmoor East, in 1918, and the 6,555-yard, par 72, course still is the sternest of the three. Robert Trent Jones designed Broadmoor West (6,109 yards, par 72), and Edwin Seay and Arnold Palmer designed Broadmoor South in 1976 (6,277 yards, par 72). Golfers playing here for the first time are delighted to discover that at this altitude the rarefied air gives them extra yardage.

There are 16 tennis courts, two in a heated bubble, facilities for horseback riding, a trap and skeet range, a ski area with a double chair lift, a 3,000-foot run with a 600-foot vertical drop, the Winter House with an excellent restaurant, and a popular ski school. In the summer, a popular pastime is the 2,600-foot Alpine Slide. All year round, ice skating brings devotees to the World Arena. The list is almost endless: if it can be enjoyed at any resort, chances are it will be found at the Broadmoor.

One of the most popular spots is the Golden Bee, an English pub in the new Convention Center. The bar and all the furnishings were salvaged from a London pub and brought here. A honky-tonk piano brings back memories of the gold rush days at Cripple Creek, just as memories are everywhere at The Broadmoor. At every turn, there is something that reminds one that The Broadmoor was the extension of one intelligent, caring man with a vision of excellence. And that is what great resorts are all about.

ARIZONA

BILTMORE

The Arizona Biltmore (overleaf) manages to be pure Art Deco and recall the temples of the Aztecs, all at the same time. Camelback Mountain is the backdrop to these golfers (left). To the left of the palm can be seen the mountain's famous Praying Monk. It is only fitting that a classic resort would attract classic motor cars such as this vintage MG.

ARIZONA BILTMORE

When Phoenix businessmen Charles and Warren MacArthur decided to build a luxury resort in the late 1920s, they chose as an architect their brother, Albert Chase MacArthur. After all, their mother's family was putting up the money and Albert had been an apprentice to Frank Lloyd Wright at the master's Oak Park, Illinois, workshop. Albert MacArthur soon talked Mr. Wright into becoming an unofficial consultant on the project and together they completed the Arizona Biltmore, one of the handsomest buildings in the country, set in 39 acres of former desert with views of Camelback Mountain. It opened in 1929, an event remembered as the most glamorous in the history of the state. The rich and the famous came and liked what they saw. The resort seemed destined for success.

But a few months after the opening the stock market crashed, and the fortunes of the resort plummeted. It was purchased by a neighbor, Chicago chewing gum magnate William Wrigley. He wintered in a rambling mansion on a hill overlooking the Arizona Biltmore, and thought that if he owned the resort it would both protect his adjacent 1,200 acres and provide a convenient place for his many visitors to stay. During the Depression, Mr. Wrigley paid the resort's operating deficits with a personal check.

The hotel is a brilliant building, one of the finest surviving examples of Art Deco architecture anywhere. It is built of concrete blocks molded with intricate details and patterns. In both materials and design, the four-story hotel and the additions blend harmoniously with the environment. In every way, the Arizona Biltmore is so representative of the work and architectural philosophy of Frank Lloyd Wright that from the beginning a controversy has raged over who really was responsible for what. Charles MacArthur wrote in 1956 that Mr. Wright had "nothing whatever" to

do with the design of the hotel. Mr. Wright's only comment was that "the building speaks for itself." Until his death in 1959, Frank Lloyd Wright was not credited, historically or legally, with the design. In a curious way, the matter was further complicated by a fire.

A welder's torch touched off a fire in the hotel that destroyed the fourth floor and the roof. The furnishings on the floors below were ruined by smoke and water. Only two weeks before, Talley Industries had purchased the resort from the Wrigleys. The company brought in Taliesin Associated Architects, of the Frank Lloyd Wright Foundation, from nearby Scottsdale to rebuild and redecorate. In researching the project, Taliesin found Frank Lloyd Wright's original sketches, so precisely detailing the finished building as to suggest Mr. Wright may have been the designer.

The Taliesin architects also found original designs for carpeting, drapery, and furniture, most of which had never been produced. They now are used throughout. A design for a stained glass mural was executed and now graces the lobby foyer. The new carpeting in the public areas of the main hotel was originally designed by Mr. Wright for his Imperial Hotel in Tokyo. The drapes and bedspreads in the guest rooms, geometric patterns of orange and greens, also are adapted from an original Frank Lloyd Wright design. The decor and furnishings throughout the resort now are both luxuriously beautiful and absolutely consistent with the original concept.

A Canadian investment group, Rostland Corporation, purchased the Arizona Biltmore and launched an expansion program. A second wing containing 120 guest rooms was added, matching in form and placement a similar addition completed in 1975. A 39,000-square-foot conference center, also designed by the Taliesin group, was completed in 1979. In all, some $40 million has been

The main dining room at the Arizona Biltmore is suitably majestic (left). The vast ceiling in the Aztec Lounge is covered with gold leaf (below). Original craftsmen came out of retirement to supervise its refurbishment.

spent on the resort since the 1973 fire.

Two public rooms are particularly noteworthy. The Aztec Lounge, and the rest of the main hotel share "the largest gold ceiling in the world." After the fire, two of the original artisans were summoned from retirement to teach 15 young workers how to apply the gold leaf to the 38,000-square-foot ceiling. The Orangerie, the resort's gourmet restaurant, replaced a cocktail lounge after the fire. It has eight specially designed glass chandeliers that hang like stalactites, softly lighting the room. Connoisseurs of high Art Deco will take particular delight in the two huge murals in the main dining room, the Gold Room, depicting fanciful Indian ceremonial scenes.

It is now practically a foregone conclusion that the Arizona Biltmore will pick up the lion's share of the awards in Phoenix area restaurant competitions. A guest soon learns why. Executive Chef Segbert Wendler has an array of Gold Room specialties—grilled breast of pheasant, lamb chops Cashmire, Dover sole Marguery, and crab legs aux fines herbes; such desserts as kiwi yogurt cake, and souffle Frangelica, to name a few. For a change of pace, excellent beef is served at the Adobe Steakhouse to the accompaniment of a classic Spanish guitar. The Adobe, at the golf clubhouse, also is open for breakfast and lunch. Lunch is served, too, at the Cabana Club next to the mammoth swimming pool.

The golf club is across the road from the hotel and offers

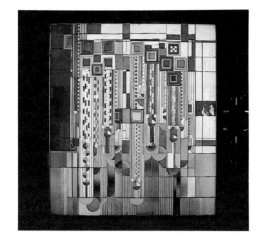

A stained glass design by Frank Lloyd Wright graces the hotel's lobby (above left). And what did you think a cowboy played golf in (below left)? An intricate pattern in concrete was utilized throughout the resort, a hallmark of the designs of Mr. Wright (below). Chess players can think big with this outsized outdoor set (bottom). The amenities of the Arizona Biltmore rival those of any resort in the world.

guests two challenging courses. The old course is the Adobe, a 6,440-yard, par 72, 1928 design by William Bell. Bill Johnson, longtime golf director here, designed the new Links course which winds around in back of the hotel. The Links, a 6,397-yard, par 72 excursion, is more rolling, narrower, and has more water hazards than does the Adobe. A dividend for golfers on either course is the chance to see some of Phoenix's finest houses along the fairways. The resort's tennis center has 18 courts, 17 of which are lighted, and a well-stocked pro shop. There are two whirlpools and a health club with steam, sauna, and massage. In addition to the main, Catalina-tiled pool, there are two other pools. A nearby riding club has mounts and miles of bridle trails. The less energetic

may amuse themselves with shuffleboard, croquet, and lawn chess. A must for everyone is a leisurely stroll around the grounds; the gardens and landscaping are as splendid as the hotel itself.

The Arizona Biltmore is an excellent base from which to explore the wonders of Arizona—the Grand Canyon, Sunset Crater, the Sedona-Oak Creek Canyon area, Montezuma Castle at Jerome, and the Casa Grande National Monument near Coolidge. For exploration of a different sort, the nearby Biltmore Shopping Center has shops that will appeal to the most discriminating.

Now ably managed by Westin Hotels, the Arizona Biltmore stands in the first rank of American resorts. It is unique, and provides its guests a uniquely satisfying experience.

103

THE WIGWAM

The red rock country (overleaf) is an easy
drive from the Wigwam.
The Territorial style cottages
are exceptionally comfortable (top).
A couple in the Owl cocktail lounge relax
after a day in the sun (above). The
Goodyear blimp is no stranger to
the Wigwam (right). The resort is
owned and operated by the tire company.

Cotton begat the Wigwam and this display in the lobby commemorates the happy fact (right). The golf courses have their share of water hazards and then some (far right). Seventy acres of luxury, the Wigwam has everything for a guest seeking the ultimate Western holiday

THE WIGWAM

Few remember how bad tires were in the early years of this century. A motor trip of several hundred miles without tire failure was an event. Trucks and buses ran on solid rubber tires which limited their speed to 20 miles an hour. The problem was tire body strength; the answer was tire cord of long-staple cotton, then raised only in Egypt and the Sea Islands of Georgia. But World War I cut off the supply of Egyptian cotton, and boll weevils were ruining the Sea Islands crop. The Department of Agriculture reported that southern Arizona might be suitable for growing long-staple cotton. The Goodyear Tire & Rubber acquired several large ranches in an attempt to grow its own cotton.

The experiment was a success. America rolled on better tires, a community sprang up to serve the cotton-growing area, and Goodyear built an Organization House in 1918 for its visiting executives and business guests. The community became Litchfield Park, named for Paul W. Litchfield, long-time president and board chairman of Goodyear. The Organization House became the Wigwam, opening to the public on Thanksgiving Day 1929 with room for 24 guests. A nine-hole golf course was added the following year, expanded to 18 holes in 1941, and the guest capacity grew to 100 by the start of World War II. During the war, the Wigwam was leased by the Army to house military personnel stationed at nearby Luke Field. The resort was greatly expanded afterward, tennis courts and two new golf courses were added, but the Wigwam retained its Territorial-style look.

The Wigwam is on 70 beautifully landscaped acres, an island of casual luxury in the middle of some 14,000 Goodyear acres. The Main Lodge contains the public rooms—the excellent Terrace Dining Room, a comfortable cocktail lounge called The Owl, a library, a card room with several fireplaces and easy chairs nearby that invite lounging—all attractively decorated in desert colors: shades of browns and oranges. Luncheon buffets are served by the

free-form swimming pool just outside the lodge.

The adobe guest lodges are scattered around the grounds. They have private entrances and patios, dressing rooms, refrigerators, bars and fireplaces. Fresh flowers complement their attractive decor.

One major reason everything runs so smoothly at the Wigwam is Clark "Corky" Corbett, vice president and general manager. He started here in 1955 at age 18 as a busboy. His rise to the top included stints as pool attendant, butcher's helper, cook, front desk clerk, night auditor, assistant manager, and night manager.

There are three golf courses to choose from, two Robert Trent Jones courses at the Goodyear Golf & Country Club, and a newer Robert F. Lawrence course, the Goodyear West, across the road. The 7,220-yard, par-72 Gold is as fine a course as there is in the Phoenix area. Nine holes have water traps and there are doglegs and trees galore. The par-70 Blue is shorter at 6,107 yards and looks much easier than it is. A golfer who can't hit straight consistently and read tricky greens will be in trouble there from start to finish. On the third course, five lakes and the stream that joins them provide Goodyear West with more than its share of water holes. The 6,861, par-72 course is a more open course than either the Blue or the Gold. The Tennis Centre has eight Plexipave courts, six of which are lighted, a lounge and all the modern teaching appurtenances. Saddle horses are available and breakfast rides are popular. There are stagecoach and hay wagon excursions and, once a week, a steak cookout with all the Western trimmings. There are supervised activities for children.

In the lobby of the Main Lodge now is a silver bowl containing shoots of cotton, their bolls burst open, white and fluffy. The Wigwam remembers its roots. And when the Goodyear board of directors meets here, another symbol of the resort's origins is much in evidence—the Goodyear blimp hovering overhead.

INN

The fun is inside as Camelback lights up the night sky (overleaf). The distinctive shape of Camelback Mountain is in the background (top). Unwinding with a view in the whirlpool (above). The lush green of the course can make one forget that this is the desert (right).

A fountain welcomes Camelback guests (left). The inn is reminiscent of the Old West. Once alone in the desert, Camelback now is part of rich, thriving Scottsdale, a Phoenix suburb.

CAMELBACK INN

The rich and the famous have been coming to Camelback Inn since it was built in 1936. Gregory Peck honeymooned here. Lt. John F. Kennedy recuperated here in 1945 from the injuries he sustained in the sinking of PT 109. Bernard Baruch was a frequent guest, so were Bette Davis and Mary Martin. The Shah of Iran gave his fellow guests a scare by his reckless horseback rides through the mountains. Neighbor Barry Goldwater made his election-night headquarters here in 1964. The miraculous climate was a factor, an average of 320 days of sunshine a year, as was the inn's setting at the base of Mummy Mountain, 120 acres that overlook famed Camelback Mountain. But the real reason for the success of Camelback and the fanatical loyalty of its guests was the personality of its founder, Jack Stewart.

Mr. Stewart was the young manager at the Wigwam in Litchfield Park and he had an itch for a place of his own. Enough people believed in him sufficiently to lend him the money to buy the land for a few dollars an acre, and build the adobe main structure and the first guest cottages. Camelback opened in 1936 and, despite the depression, quickly was a success. Mr. Stewart and his wife Louise were involved with the inn to a degree almost unimaginable today. No detail was too small to escape their attention. No effort was too great to make a guest feel at home. They took delight in introducing guests to one another, and for decades Camelback was a sort of extended family for thousands of regular guests.

Everything at Camelback is in the Spanish Southwest style. The adobe guest houses all have private entrances, refrigerators in the warm, comfortable rooms, and private patios or balconies. The suites are two-leveled with wet bars, loft bedrooms, and most have private swimming pools. The main building houses the Chaparral and Navajo dining rooms, a snack bar called the Cactus Patch, the Oasis Lounge, and La Chaparrell where there is nightly dancing. There are beautiful out-sized swimming pools in front and in back of the inn.

The Camelback Golf Club is three miles away and has two excellent courses. The original course, the Padre, is a 6,584-yard, par 71 Robert F. Lawrence design with elevated greens and trees. The newer course, Indian Bend, is longer at 7,030, par 72, and winds around the Indian Bend Wash. The tee markers on both courses are kneeling camels. There also is the pitch-and-putt executive course. Tennis players have ten all-weather courts at their disposal. Horses may be rented and the trails afford spectacular views of the mountains and the Phoenix skyline.

The high season is winter and that is when the rich and famous come to play. A social director is on hand to solve problems. There is free transportation to a shopping center as elegant as any between Fifth Avenue and Rodeo Drive. Sightseeing trips can be arranged, even air tours of the Grand Canyon. Once a week there is an outdoor steak fry. It's held at sunset, a few minutes up the slopes of Mummy Mountain, and really recaptures the feel of the Old West.

Marriott acquired Camelback in 1967 and has spent a lot of effort and money expanding its facilities and keeping everything up to snuff. The resort's high rating is testimony to Marriott's commitment to quality. Some of the intimacy of the old days is gone but the Stewarts were a very tough act to follow.

111

SUN VALLEY

Skiing is a way of life at Sun Valley (overleaf). The main dining room of the Lodge is the setting for a meal in the grand tradition (opposite). The more informal Ram Restaurant is a popular apres-ski rendezvous (left). There are seven restaurants at Sun Valley, offering guests a wide range of dining choices—from *haute cuisine* to a piping hot fondue.

SUN VALLEY

Averell Harriman had learned to ski in Europe, and he believed that if he created a ski resort in the American West it would build passenger traffic on his Union Pacific Railroad. He sent a family friend, Austrian ski expert Count Felix Schaffgotsch, to search for a suitable location. The count visited Mount Rainier, Mount Hood, Jackson Hole, and Lake Tahoe, among others. One by one, he rejected them: too high, too windy, too many weekend skiers, too far from the railroad. Then someone suggested Ketchum, Idaho, an old, worn-out mining town, whose population by 1936 had dwindled to 270. After seeing the area, the count wrote to Harriman, "It contains more delightful features for a winter sports center than any other place I have seen in the United States, Switzerland or Austria."

Within days, Harriman had arrived on his private railroad car and purchased a 4,300-acre ranch. Three million depression dollars were budgeted for construction. The 45-year-old Harriman's next move was to hire Steve Hannagan, whose publicity skills had lifted Miami Beach from obscurity. Hannagan came reluctantly: he hated cold weather and despised winter sports. Paradoxically, his antipathy was the spark that was needed. He sold Harriman on naming the resort Sun Valley; he insisted on a heated, glass-enclosed, outdoor swimming pool; fine food formally served; an orchestra for nightly dancing; and, most significantly, some way to get skiers to the top of the mountain sitting down. "This is one place," said Hannagan, "where roughing it must be a luxury."

Union Pacific engineers made the first workable ski lift, adapting a device used in Central America to transport bunches of bananas from a mountain to a rail siding below. By Christmas of 1936, Sun Valley had its ski lift, a heated outdoor pool, an ice rink, a ski school, and a 220-room lodge built out of poured concrete, then stencilled and stained to resemble logs. The first guests danced to Eddy Duchin and his orchestra.

A few months later, Hannagan talked Paramount into filming the mountain scenes for Claudette Colbert's "I Met Him In Paris" at Sun Valley. Set designers built an alpine village around the Lodge. This so pleased Harriman that he asked them to design an inn to accommodate those unable to afford the Lodge. It was later flanked by a restaurant, an opera house, and a second outdoor heated swimming pool. The following year chalets were built where college students could rent a bunk bed for one dollar a night.

Hannagan then lured Ernest Hemingway and his wife into becoming semi-permanent guests. At Sun Valley, he completed "For Whom the Bell Tolls." Pictures filled the press of his welcoming to Sun Valley Gary Cooper and Ingrid Bergman, the stars of the movie version of his novel. Hemingway lent a masculine panache to the resort that lingers to this day. No skier himself, Hemingway loved the mountains and the bird and big-game hunting he found there. He bought a home nearby and lived there on and off until his tragic death.

The publicity masterstroke came in 1941, with "Sun Valley Serenade," starring Sonja Henie, John Payne, Milton Berle, and the Glenn Miller Orchestra. Hans Hauser, head of the resort's ski school, skied for Payne, schussing behind a tree where Payne would then take over for the close-ups. Ms. Henie's ski sequences were

performed by a local teenager, Gretchen Fraser, later to become the first American—male or female—to win an Olympic gold medal for alpine racing. To this day, first-time guests arrive saying, "We saw 'Sun Valley Serenade' years ago and we've been wanting to come here ever since."

Sun Valley always has been a watering hole for celebrities. Rose Kennedy's children learned to ski here; so did the Shah of Iran. President Truman fished in the lake during his 1948 visit. Marilyn Monroe stayed at the Lodge while filming "Bus Stop" on location in Ketchum. Groucho Marx was married in suite 305. The public rooms are filled with photographs of Hollywood's greats and near-greats at play: Clark Gable, Loretta Young, Tyrone Power, Jimmy Stewart, Ralph Bellamy, June Allyson, Ann Sothern and oh-so-many-others.

Sun Valley now is a year-round resort. There is an excellent 6,620-yard, par-71, Robert Trent Jones, Jr. golf course, 18 tennis courts, special "Young Summer" and "Teen Summer" programs for the younger guests, horseback riding on beautiful mountain trails, trap and skeet, whitewater float trips on the Salmon River, bicycling, soaring, sailing on Sun Valley Lake, hiking in the Sawtooth National Recreational Area, a diverse program of arts, crafts and humanities, and some of the best trout fishing anywhere. As a counterpart to outdoor swimming in the winter, there is outdoor skating in the summer. On weekends there are ice shows, starring some of the world's top professional skaters.

Despite the glories of summer, it is winter when Sun Valley really shines. Bald Mountain, "Baldy" to the knowledgable, couldn't be a better ski mountain if it had been built to order. The

top is like a giant ice cream cone, skiable on three sides. The ski school begins instruction on Dollar Mountain but by the end of the first week, pupils are skiing Baldy, a 9,360-foot peak with 12 chair lifts, three restaurants, 750 acres of groomed runs and trails, and a drop of some 3,600 feet. One unique aspect of Sun Valley is that the resort and ski areas are managed by the same corporation. The slopes and trails are groomed every night, and, even on the busiest days, the wait for a lift rarely exceeds five minutes.

Sun Valley was purchased in 1977 by R. Earl Holding. His first move was to stop land sales and the construction of condominiums which were threatening to change the character of the resort. He replaced old lifts, installed new ones, planted 5,000 trees and is refurbishing both the Lodge and the Inn. Particular attention has been paid to dining. The main dining room at the Lodge has been elevated to world class, both in decor and cuisine. In the Alpine village, the Ram offers steaks and chops and a delicious pan-fried rainbow trout with lemon butter and capers. Penguini's offers a dozen varieties of pizza and other Italian specialties. The Konditorei has a mouth-watering display of freshly baked breads, pastries and desserts. Winter guests are taken by sleighs across moonlit snowy fields to feast on barbecue by a roaring fire at Trail Creek Cabin, an old hunting lodge where Hemingway and Gary Cooper used to swap yarns at the bar.

In the nearly 50 years since Averell Harriman built his dream resort, ski resorts have sprung up throughout the country. All owe a debt to Sun Valley for showing what a ski resort could be. None, however, has come up with anything quite as splendid.

HARRAH'S

The impressionistic beauty of Lake Tahoe is unmatched (overleaf). Lake and mountains are visible from all the guest rooms at Harrah's (left). In the mammoth casino there's action around around the clock. There are more gaming tables and slot machines here than in any other casino in the world. Players relax with big-time entertainment. Frank Sinatra, Don Rickles and Bill Cosby are all regulars.

HARRAH'S HOTEL AND CASINO

Gambling is as much a part of the warp and woof of the American West as cowboy boots or cattle drives. And for those who equate a perfect holiday with the excitement of the gaming tables, no place in the country quite compares with Harrah's on the Nevada shore of Lake Tahoe. The casino has the largest assemblage of tables and slot machines in the world, and a player's chances are as good here as at any other casino and better than at most. The South Shore Room features the cream in night club entertainers—Frank Sinatra, Barbara Mandrell, Don Rickles, Joan Rivers, Bill Cosby—and doesn't impose a cover charge. The hotel is the only one in Nevada Mobil rates at five stars and one of eight such in the country. The Summit Restaurant on the top floors offers a breathtaking panorama and, unlike most restaurants with a view, merits its four-star rating. Then there's the setting.

Lake Tahoe is almost too beautiful, too theatrical. It is an alpine lake, the largest on the continent, fed from the mountains that surround it—a Cecil B. DeMille lake wrapped in soaring Dino De Laurentiis mountains. The statistics are worthy of note: it is 12 miles wide, 22 miles long, some 6,200 feet above sea level, 99.994 per cent pure. Its bottom plunges to 1,645 feet, and if it ever sprang a leak it could cover the entire state of California with 14 inches of water. There are 36 beaches and picnic areas, 12 golf courses, 23 marinas, 11 riding stables, 10 tennis facilities, 2,300 campsites, 32 recognized cross-country ski areas, 20 ski resorts, including Heavenly, whose 20 square miles of trails and open slopes make it the largest ski area in the country.

The 18-story, 540-room hotel has some impressive statistics, too. Each guest room includes two complete bathrooms, three televisions and three telephones. Angled windows give a view of both the lake and the mountains. In the rooms a computerized beverage machine will dispense everything from martinis to champagne at the push of a button. There's a fresh rose in each room, the beds are turned down at night, and a foil-wrapped chocolate is on the pillow. Butler service is part of the good life in the suites on the 16th floor. A former "Man Friday" to Winthrop Rockefeller supervises services that range from sewing on a button to handling a small dinner party. Besides the exquisite Summit, guests may dine in The Forest, a second rooftop restaurant, featuring a different "theme" buffet each night, Seafood Cove, or Friday's Station Steak House on the casino level, or take in the dinner show at the South Shore Room. A viable alternative is 24-hour room service. A heated swimming pool in a plexiglass dome, Jacuzzi, and health club are there to revive the weary gamesman.

Sixty miles away in Reno is Harrah's Automobile Collection. Nearly 1,000 cars are on display, all carefully preserved or authentically restored. In the movie "Annie," Daddy Warbucks drove a 1929 Duesenberg Dual Cowl Phaeton and a 1930 du Pont Royal Town Car from the collection.

Harrah's, now owned by Holiday Inns, Inc., is the legacy of Bill Harrah, a Reno entrepreneur who opened a bingo game there in 1937. It closed after two months, but the next year he tried again, and never looked back. Over the years he showed how Lady Luck should be courted—in style.

The *maitre d'* at the elegant Summit restaurant atop Harrah's prepares *peche flambé* (far left); Sparkling slot machines await customers in the casino (left); Lake Tahoe is 99.994 per cent pure and remarkably clear (below left). By popular belief the lake is bottomless, actually the deepest point is 1,645 feet.

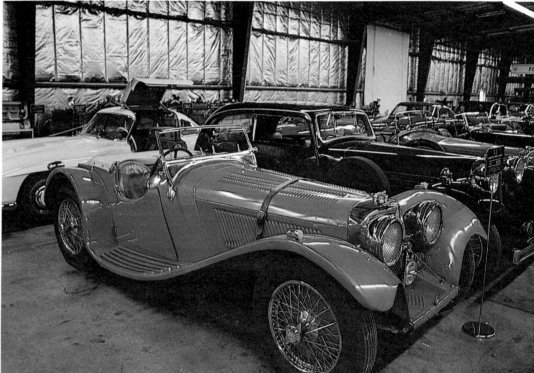

The graceful swan on the radiator identifies the classic Hispano-Suiza, a favorite of European royalty (top). A vintage MG-TC is one of more than a thousand cars on display at Harrah's Automobile Collection (above). The first car produced by the great Augie and Fred Dusenberg was this spiffy 1906 Mason runabout (left).

123

PEBBLE BEACH

A surfer (overleaf) comes in for a closer look at the action on the 18th green. Near the Lodge on the 17-Mile Drive is the Lone Cypress (opposite), one of the most recognizable landmarks in the country. At the Beach and Tennis Club, the top of a grand piano plays along with the lovely view (left). The Lodge first was built as an overnight stop for those driving carriages around the 17-Mile Drive.

THE LODGE AT PEBBLE BEACH

In California's empire-building days, they were the Big Four: Leland Stanford, Collis P. Huntington, Mark Hopkins, and Charles Crocker. Mr. Crocker was the engineer, the man who got things done. And when their Central Pacific Railroad was finished and linked to the Union Pacific to span the West, he quickly became restless. His mood changed, however, on his first visit to the small fishing village of Monterey. He immediately sensed the recreational possibilities of the beautiful bay. He and his partners took over the narrow-gauge railroad that served Monterey, and bought up large tracts of land. On the north side of the bay, Mr. Crocker built an impressive hotel, three stories high, 300 feet long, with turrets and towers and long verandas. It opened in 1880 as the Hotel Del Monte. To help attract guests, the railroad was rebuilt to standard gauge all the way to San Francisco.

The Del Monte Hotel became the focus of Mr. Crocker's life, and he spent a great deal of time there. He set management policies and was a genial host. In 1887, a fire broke out and spread through the hotel. No one was injured, but the building was nearly demolished. Mr. Crocker rebuilt the Del Monte the next year, but the strain on him apparently was too much. He died at the hotel at 67 years of age of a diabetic coma. The hotel continued after his death, the managing company increasing their land holdings in the area, adding what is believed to be the first 18-hole golf course west of the Mississippi. A carriage road was built along the rugged seacoast southwest of Monterey, the 17-Mile Drive, with a pine-log lodge at Pebble Beach. The lodge was popular right from its 1908 opening, and a row of cottages were added six years later.

The railroad interests of the Big Four were sold off, but the resort interests and other properties were retained. In 1915, a Yale classmate of Mr. Crocker's grandson joined the firm: Samuel F. B. Morse, grandnephew of the inventor, a rugged six-footer who had been captain of the Yale football team. In 1919, Mr. Morse was given the task of liquidating the company's holdings, but he had other ideas. He and an associate raised the necessary capital to form Del Monte Properties Company which included the Monterey hotel, the Lodge at Pebble Beach, and the land encompassing the 17-Mile Drive. The lodge had burned down in 1917, but was rebuilt in its present form; the hotel suffered a similar fate in 1924, but also was rebuilt. In the 1920s, the rich of the San Francisco area started building homes along the 17-Mile Drive. Mr. Morse exercised control over the land development to make sure the area retained its natural beauty.

The Depression was hard on Del Monte Properties Company. Hotel business was slow, and land sales nearly disappeared. When the war came, the Navy leased the Del Monte Hotel as a pre-flight school, and hired Del Monte Properties Company to cater it for them. It became a hotel briefly after the war, but it was sold in 1946 and became the administration building of the Naval Postgraduate School.

Today the Lodge at Pebble Beach is as beautiful and fashionable as any in the country. Guests are quartered in two-story buildings near the Lodge in rooms that have balconies, fireplaces laid with logs and kindling, dressing rooms, opulent bathrooms—the rooms are in a class by themselves for comfort and taste. The Lodge itself is a model of low-key elegance. The sitting-room looks out across the 18th green of the golf course to the bay beyond. The surf rolls in, forming a white background to the lush green.

The Pebble Beach golf course is among the top courses in the world, and, arguably, the most beautiful. Considering its reputation, it comes as a surprise that it was laid out in 1916 by Jack Neville and Douglas Grant, two amateur golfers, though both had been state champions. When it was completed in 1919, it became the permanent site of the state amateur championships. But Pebble's fame has come from other tournaments. For more than three decades, it has been the home of the Crosby Pro-Am. (Bing Crosby had a home adjoining the course here for many years.) It also has hosted two U.S. amateur championships, two women's amateur championships, the 1972 and the 1982 U.S. Opens and the 1977

127

The 7th hole at Pebble (left) is one of the most magnificent in all of golf; 103 yards downhill to a green ringed by traps and the sea. The 18th hole (above) is an exciting finish, climaxing at a green tucked between the Lodge and the surf-tossed shore.

PGA championship. It was at Pebble in 1929 that Bobby Jones, the defending champion, lost the U.S. Amateur in the first round. In 1976, it was Jack Nicklaus's turn. Tied for the lead in the Crosby going into the back nine, he took a seven on the 13th, and a six on the 17th to card an 82.

The first three holes at Pebble are inland (a 373-yard par 4, a 439-yard par 5, and a 341-yard par 40) and don't suggest the beauties and perils to come. Hole four (303-yards, par 4) heads for Stillwater Cove. Miss the right bunker, and the ball is in the ocean; overshoot the green, and the ball is in a deep gully. Five (a 140-yard, par 3) requires an accurate shot through a narrow gap between clumps of trees. Six (487 yards, par 5), is long and tricky with a dog-leg to the right along the ocean. In the curve of the dog-leg, the fairway slopes down to a cliff. Seven (a 103-yard, par 3) is one of the most magnificent holes in all of golf, going downhill to a trap-ringed green sticking out in the ocean. To overclub is to lose a ball in the ocean; to hit too high is to be blown into a trap. Eight (405-yards, par 4) offers no respite, with a dog-leg right, and a cove that cuts in about 200 yards out. The green slopes to the ocean and can be lightening fast. Nine (439 yards, par 4) again hugs the shore. The second shot is particulary difficult, as a ball will roll toward the water. The green is small, and ringed with water on three sides.

The pressure continues on the back nine. The tenth (411 yards, par 4) repeats the lesson that a ball hit to the middle of the fairway will roll toward the ocean. The eleventh (384 yards, par 4) is inland but is a blind tee shot, coupled with a bunkered green. The twelfth (184-yards, par-3) is a wide-fairway beauty with a huge bunker right in front of the green. The (373-yard, par-4) thir-

A repast as splendid at the view can be
found at the Beach and Tennis Club
(opposite). A favorite watering hole
of golfers is the Tap Room (below) in
the Lodge where the walls are laden with
memorabilia from the Crosby Pro-Ams; the
golfer on the left is Ben Hogan, on the
right in plus fours is Der Bingle
himself. Mule deer have the
run of the course at nearby Spyglass.

teenth is notable for a green that pitches from left to right. The fourteenth is very long (553 yards, par 5), and some say it is the most demanding at Pebble. Few can reach the green in two, and the third shot is uphill over a giant trap. The fifteenth (366 yards, par 4) has a row of large pines on the left and the 17-Mile Drive on the right. It dog-legs slightly left. The sixteenth (366 yards, par 4) seems designed to encourage overshooting the green and into a chasm—an almost certain guarantee of a double bogey. The seventeenth (175-yard, par 3) goes back to the ocean. The green is oversized, kidney-shaped, and emminently three-puttable. The eighteenth is, simply, the greatest finishing hole in golf: a 538-yard, par 5, that runs along the ocean back to the lodge. The fairway is narrow, there's a tree smack in the middle of it, and the green is well-bunkered.

A round at Pebble Beach is a high point in the life of any golfer. Says Jack Nicklaus, "If I had only one more round of golf to play, I would choose to play it at Pebble Beach. I can't imagine anyone ever creating a finer all-round test of golf in a more sensational setting."

Guests also may play at nearby Spyglass Hill, a 6,277-yard, par-72 design by Robert Trent Jones, Sr. Spyglass is a tough course, and many rate it as difficult as Pebble Beach. The Old Del Monte Golf Course in Monterey (6,154 yards, par 72) is easy only by comparison to Pebble and Spyglass. There is another course here, Cypress Point, which is every bit the equal of Pebble Beach but is for members only. If a guest were to be invited to play Cypress, however, it would be a sacrilege to say no.

Even the most ardent golfer must pause to eat, however, and

the choices at the Lodge are excellent and varied. Overlooking the bay is the Cypress Room, a warm, elegant establishment with a continental menu. Club XIX is for true gourmets, its abalone meunière and mignonettes de veau aux chanterelles are especially recommended. For dessert, a welcome change-of-pace is fresh orange sections with almonds and Cointreau. If one is celebrating a fine golf round, there is Beluga malossol caviar and a well-chosen wine list. A light supper suggests the casual Tap Room where the walls are laden with tournament memorabilia. Late breakfasts and light lunches may be found in the Gallery, overlooking the putting green from the second-floor of the row of exclusive shops.

Recreational facilities abound. There is the Peter Hay Course, a nine-hole, par 3, course across from the golf shop. The Beach and Tennis Club has 14 courts, a heated, Olympic-size pool, children's pool, and saunas. The Equestrian Center gives private and group lessons, and escorted rides over 34 miles of trails. A parcourse is available for joggers, and fishermen may charter boats at the Monterey Marina.

Certainly, no first-time visit to Pebble Beach would be complete without a leisurely excursion around the 17-Mile Drive. A trip to the galleries and boutiques in almost-too-cute Carmel can be fun. John Steinbeck's Cannery Row in Monterey is interesting. The best side trip, though, is south past Point Lobos to the awesome Big Sur coastline, the most majestic meeting of land and sea in the country.

To think of Pebble Beach as a golf resort is to miss its essence entirely. Pebble Beach is a classic small resort which just happens to have a golf course as fine as there is.

LAS PALMAS

Two chefs seem pleased
with their efforts (left).
A mariachi band plays
for guests by the
swimming pool (below).
A feeling of Old Mexico
is part of the charm here.

The lake at Las
Palmas reflects the
palms (overleaf)
that gave the
resort its name.
From rolling fair-
ways to snowcapped
mountains, golf
at Las Palmas
is a visual treat
(opposite). The
Territorial style
dining room is
the setting for
a bounteous
brunch (right).

RANCHO LAS PALMAS

Palm Springs has a habit of being rediscovered. The first redis-
coverer was a young Army lieutenant, R. S. Williamson, in charge
of a surveying party seeking the best railway route to link the Mississippi and the Pacific. He reported passes to a desert ringed with
mountains, a band of friendly Indians living in a wild palm grove,
and a hot mineral spring filling a 30-foot pool. In 1887, the Southern Pacific established service from Yuma to Los Angeles via Palm
Springs, and the area, known to the early Indians and Mexicans
as "La Palma de la Mano de Dios (The Hollow of God's Hand),"
slowly came to life.

The next rediscoverers were Charlie Farrell and Ralph Bellamy who built their Racquet Club in 1933 and soon were introducing their fellow Hollywood luminaries to the pleasures of the
desert. With an average of 350 sunny days a year, temperatures
that range from 88° by day to 55° at night, and only 120 miles
from the movie capital, Palm Springs quickly became Hollywood's
second home. The local streets tell the story: Bob Hope Drive,
Frank Sinatra Drive, Spencer Tracy Drive, Bette Davis Way, John
Wayne Road, Rock Hudson Circle, and William Powell Road, to
name a few. Then after World War II, "The Springs," as it is
known to its affluent residents, was rediscovered by practically
everyone else, quickly becoming the greatest desert resort community in the world. Consider: there are now some 7,000 swimming pools, one for every five permanent residents, 350 tennis
courts and 40 golf courses (including former ambassador Walter
Annenberg's private course).

Of the many resorts in the desert, none offers more—or offers it all more attractively—than Rancho Las Palmas, a 26-acre
oasis on Bob Hope Drive, less than a mile from the mind-boggling
Annenberg enclave. Any resort worthy of its name has a golf
course, and Rancho Las Palmas's 27-hole Ted Robinson championship course ranks with the best. But here the golf course was
built first and the resort, a series of Spanish Mission style buildings, was woven around and through it, a fit as deft as that of Yin
and Yang. Amazingly, the golfers don't bother the non-golfers, and
vice versa; rather there is a synergism that lends the resort a special character. Nor are the tennis players shortchanged: there are
25 all-weather courts, eight lighted. Three beautifully landscaped
swimming pools with companion Jacuzzi whirlpool baths and sun-
decks compete for the enjoyment of the guests. There are 456
deluxe, oversized guest rooms and suites in the two-story buildings, each with outside entrances and a patio or balcony. All are
soundproof, with color televison and other amenities. The main
dining room is the elegant, multi-level Cabrillo. Small groups can
dine from a personally selected menu in the Cuarto del Vino, a
chic, intimate room where personal attention is unflagging. The
Sunrise Terrace is an outdoor restaurant with a marvelous view of
the mountains, and serves a bountiful buffet breakfast and lunch.
Miquel's offers dancing to a live orchestra and generous cocktails.

Rancho Las Palmas was built and is operated by Marriott,
an increasingly important factor in the fine resort field. Marriott's
rediscovery of this desert paradise was a fortunate one: Rancho Las
Palmas in five years has earned the right to stand with the best.

LA COSTA

Early morning mist lends a spectral quality to the course (overleaf). A topiary logo looks out over the manicured course. La Costa offers an array of spa and sports facilities with a healthful climate to its affluent guests.

LA COSTA HOTEL AND SPA

Once all American resorts were spas, their guests seeking rejuvenation. By the 1920's, pleasure had become an end in itself and the old spas either changed with the times or faded away. Health consciousness returned to fashion in the middle 1960's, and La Costa became the first resort to re-invent the spa. Rejuvenation now meant weight reduction and muscle toning. Under the direction of Dr. R. Philip Smith, La Costa's medical director, a series of diet regimens were prepared at the 600, 800 and 1,000-a-day calorie levels. These were coupled with modern exercise programs and a range of spa treatments—Roman baths, massage, whirlpools, luffa scrubs, herbal wraps, and saunas—and presented in the context of a luxury resort. Since La Costa, there have been imitations and variations but none produce better results nor offer so much.

Those seeking a prison farm atmosphere for weight reduction won't find it at La Costa. No whips crack; no instructors bellow. There is a quiet, cheerful, adult atmosphere in both the men's and women's spas. Those who associate weight reduction with hunger pains and unappetizing meals are in for a surprise, too. Even the 600-calorie-a-day meals are tasty, filling and well presented. Those on diets eat in a special area of the main dining room, and the casual observer would be hard put to see the difference between this area and the area for the non-dieting guests. La Costa is truly co-ed, couples come with one or the other using the spas, or both enjoying the sybaritic life. And, importantly, there is a crossover: spa guests may use all the recreational facilities of the resort; resort guests may arrange to use whatever spa facilities appeal to them.

It's fortunate the low-calorie meals are so good, or the dining opportunities at La Costa would prove irresistible. Besides the Continental Dining Room, there is the Steak House, the Seville Room, offering Italian specialities, and Pisces, which serves up such delectables as bouillabaisse, fillet of sole Veronique, and Maine lobster. There are a variety of choices in accommodations, too. The Chateaux have wet bars, powder rooms, and a combination living-bedroom with queen-size beds which disappear electrically into the walls. Cottage suites are commodious, the executive homes adjoining the golf course even more so.

Golf is a major attraction and the course designed by Dick Wilson is the permanent home of the PGA MONY Tournament of Champions. There are three nines: Green and Gold are 6,855 yards, par 72; Orange is 2,986, par 36. They may be played in any combination but Green and Gold is the tournament course. The seventh on the Green is a delight, a par three with a tiny blue lake and a double waterfall. There also are 25 hard-surfaced tennis courts, including a 4,000-seat exhibition court, all under the supervision of past master Pancho Segura, the long-time coach of Jimmy Connors. Swimmers have four heated pools to choose from in the central area and a nearby Beach Club. Equestrians may board their horses at the Saddle Club, which has a show ring and a choice of interesting trails.

La Costa is two hours south of Los Angeles and attracts its share of Hollywood personalities. It attracts more than its share of guests who like to come home from a luxurious holiday looking and feeling better.

A golfer putting (left), while his lovely counterpart luxuriates in a spa whirlpool (below). Both the men's and women's spas are models of design and equipment. Under the leadership of Pancho Segura, La Costa draws world-class tennis tournaments to its center court (lower left.) The strictest spa program includes time to relax as the two maidens at the pool charmingly attest

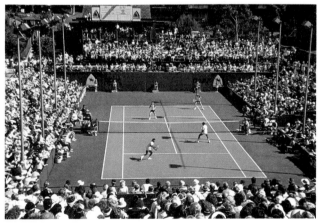

CORONADO

Unbelievable as it seems the Coronado had no architect and only the roughest of plans (overleaf). Palm tree is framed in the window of the elegant dining room (opposite). The interior court of the hotel has a charming gazebo in the middle (left). The builders learned as they went along. Workmanship at the rear is less sophisticated than in the tower section at front.

HOTEL DEL CORONADO

A retired railroad executive and a piano manufacturer went rabbit hunting on an uninhabited, unnamed, wind-blown peninsula near San Diego, sensed that it might have development possibilities, and bought the peninsula and nearby North Island in 1885 for $110,000. The retired railroader, Elisha S. Babcock, and H. L. Story of the Story & Clark Piano Company picked the name Coronado from a naming contest. They started selling lots and soon were taking in from $100,000 to $400,000 a month. They wanted to build a grand hotel and brought in railroad engineers—the Reid brothers, James, Merritt and Watson—to build it for them. They also knew just what they wanted, a hotel that would be "the talk of the Western world."

This is how they described it to their builders:

It would be built around a court . . . a garden of tropical trees, shrubs and flowers, with pleasant paths . . . balconies should look down on this court from every story. From the south end, the foyer should open to Glorietta Bay with verandas for rest and promenade. On the ocean corner, there should be a pavilion tower, and northward along the ocean, a colonade, terraced in grass to the beach. The dining wing should project at an angle from the southeast corner of the court and be almost detached, to give full value to the view of the ocean, bay and city.

That was sufficient for the Reid brothers. They made some rough drawings. Both a railroad and a ferryboat system had to be built to handle the lumber, building materials, fixtures, furnishings and laborers involved in the project. All the lumber was transported by ship from northern California. The Chinese Six Companies of San Francisco provided most of the nearly 2,000 laborers.

A brick kiln, metal shop, foundry and lumber planing mill were constructed at the site. Ground-breaking ceremonies were held in March 1887. Less than a year later the first guests checked in, although the hotel wasn't totally completed for another two years. This was a prodigious feat—the roof required two million shingles, and the Del Coronado was the first hotel west of the Mississippi to be lit entirely by electricity. (A back-up gas illumination system was installed but never used.) The hotel cost $600,000 to build and $400,000 to furnish. A special train from the east brought in 324 people who formed the hotel staff, including the celebrated French chef de cuisine Frederick Pierre Compagnon, who had been lured away from the Grand Hotel at Mackinac Island. It was a large staff for 399 guest rooms.

The hotel captivated society from the start. Local newspapers chronicled the arrival of the "floury Pillsburys, the yeasty Fleischmanns and the billiard-rich Bensingers." Among the guests over the years have been 11 U.S. presidents: Harrison, McKinley, Taft, Wilson, Franklin D. Roosevelt, Eisenhower, Johnson, Kennedy, Nixon, Carter and Reagan. No visitor, however, has ever created a sensation to equal the April 1920 visit of Edward, Prince of Wales, the first member of British royalty to travel to the West Coast. He arrived on board the H.M.S. Renown, and a day of ceremonies and festivities was crowned by the mayor's dinner for the prince, and a reception and ball, both events held at the Hotel del Coronado. It was at the reception that he met his future duchess, then Mrs. Earl Spencer, wife of a naval aviator stationed at North Island. To mark the occasion, the hotel commissioned a full set of china emblazoned with the imperial crown for its 1,000-seat

grand dining room, later renamed the Crown Room.

Hollywood knew a good thing when it saw it, and a number of movies have been filmed at the resort. The first was the 1927 epic "The Flying Fleet," starring Ramon Navarro and Anita Page. The most memorable, however, was Billy Wilder's "Some Like It Hot," a 1958 hit with Marilyn Monroe, Tony Curtis and Jack Lemmon. Few who have seen it have forgotten the chase scene across the hotel roof.

More recently, it was the setting for "Stunt Man" with Peter O'Toole. The filming was so traumatic, with a false turret being blown up and a real stunt man fracturing his leg, that the hotel passed up the chance to star in the movie version of a novel written about it, Richard Matheson's "Bid Time Return." The setting in the screenplay was changed to the Grand Hotel at Mack-

inac and it was filmed as "Somewhere in Time."

The exterior of the Hotel del Coronado is virtually the same today as when it was built, a classic example of Queen Anne architecture. It rambles, its red roof a melange of towers and turrets and dormers, looking for all the world like an American version of a Ruritanian castle. The guest rooms have all been remodeled and refurbished. The Prince of Wales Grille, a gourmet dining room, was opened in 1970. Three years later, the new 208-room Ocean Towers and a 16,000-square foot convention facility were added. In 1979, a poolside addition was opened containing 96 guest rooms. The Lobby Bar also is new although perfectly in keeping with the Victorian style of the other public rooms.

Two rooms at the del Coronado deserve special attention. The Crown Room, which sits under the hotel's dome is 120 feet

At the nearby marina, the boathouse now is a fashionable restaurant (opposite). From the beach, the tower is a beacon to guests (left). The bay is a mecca for sailors (right). The etched glass entrance doors were installed for a movie filmed at the del Coronado, but became so popular they were left in place (below). Hollywood has been using the resort as a setting for movies for 50 years.

in diameter and chandeliers in the form of crowns hang from its 33-foot ceiling. Huge wooden trusses in the tower support the ceiling so that no pillars are necessary. The ceiling is of natural-finish sugarpine, fitted together pegs. The Crown Room seats 800 comfortably with room left over for a dance floor. Charles Lindbergh was feted here in 1927 while a replica of his Spirit of St. Louis circled the ceiling. The Ballroom is equally magnificent, 120 feet in diameter with six crystal chandeliers. Recently renovated, the Ballroom is the setting for many of San Diego's important society functions. Also a guest should not leave The del Coronado without stopping by the peaceful Ocean Terrace bar. This mahogany bar was built in Pennsylvania in 1895, taken apart, and sent here by ship around the tip of South America. A favorite drink here is the Crown Jewel, a mixture of white rum and orange juice.

A nine-hole golf course was built along with the hotel but was lost to developers over the years. Guests now play at the excellent Coronado Municipal Golf Course, a few blocks away. Other activities abound. There are seven all-weather lighted tennis courts on the ocean side of the hotel, two extra-large swimming pools, acres of white sand beach, a nearby marina where deep-sea fishing and sailing may be arranged, bicycle and jogging trails, and a well equipped spa. San Diego is next door and has a variety of attractions, including a world-famous zoo, Mission Bay Aquatic Park, and Balboa Park. Mexico is about a half-hour drive away.

As if this weren't enough, the Hotel del Coronado enjoys what many believe is the finest climate in the country. The average monthly temperature ranges from a high in August of 74.6° Fahrenheit to a low in January of 62.9°.

145

A stroll on the beach at Wailea can be heaven (overleaf). Warm tropic sun and cool water are a tempting combination (opposite). Each guest room is complete with terrace and view (right). What is an island resort without tall drinks and pretty girls (above right). A mother's thumb is reassuring when first venturing into the water (below right). Offshore coral reefs teem with marine life.

WESTIN WAILEA BEACH

Humpback whales, nearly 100 of them, migrate from Alaskan waters to the bay here, leviathans weighing as much as 50 tons, who seem to enjoy going through their antics for Wailea Beach guests. The whales have impeccable taste—there is no more idyllic spot in the Hawaiian Islands. The slopes of Mount Haleakala, a dormant volcano, ease down to the blue waters of the Pacific. A few miles off shore is the sunken volcanic isle of Molokini, and coral reefs beckon the snorkelers and scuba divers.

Wailea Beach takes full advantage of its spectacular location, and adds something of its own to the environment. All of its 350 rooms have private lanais and more than half look out at the ocean. The rest face the mountain or the lush tropical garden that surrounds the hotel. There are two waterfalls, a stream, a tranquil pond and a profusion of tropical plantings: 50 varieties of banana trees, Be-still trees with bell-shaped yellow flowers, Kukui or candlenut trees, Royal Poincianas, African Tulip Trees with fiery orange flowers, orchids and six varieties of ginger. At the Maui Onion, the restaurant by the swimming pool, the overhead trellises are festooned with the bell-shaped flowers of the Thunbergia vine. This is landscape architecture at its best. A highpoint of the garden is a contemporary statue of the god Maui pulling the Hawaiian Islands up from the sea.

Since its opening in the fall of 1978, the Wailea Beach has achieved recognition as one of Hawaii's outstanding resorts. It is the only resort on Maui and one of three in the islands to receive the Five Diamond Award from the American Automobile Association. Raffles', its gourmet restaurant, has received its share of awards as well. Executive Chef Neil Sint-Nicolaas offers such spe-

cialties as fresh vegetable tempura with mulligatawny dip, roast young duckling with green peppercorns and kiwi fruit, and interesting treatments of the native fish: opakapaka (a delicious cousin to red snapper), ulua, and mahimahi. In the Palm Court, the main dining room, guests are offered a choice of traditional specialties or a buffet which offers the cuisine of a different country each evening. A traditional Hawaiian luau with live entertainment is a weekly feature in the garden. The Lost Horizon offers music and dancing until the wee hours.

There is plenty to do at the beach—sailboating, windsurfing, snorkeling and scuba diving. It's worth getting up in the dark to be taken up to the 10,000-foot summit crater of Mount Halekala to watch the sunrise paint it a thousand different hues.

For the more traditionally athletic, the Wailea Tennis Club has three grass and 11 Laykold courts. The 1,000-seat stadium court is the site of the Wailea Pro Tennis Classic—the Hawaiian stop of the Volvo Grand Prix circuit. Jack Snyder designed Wailea's two 18-hole golf courses. The wide fairways of the 6,291, par 72 Blue Course are forgiving but its 72 bunkers and four lakes are not. The Orange Course, 6,405, par 72, is the tougher of the two with more dog-legs and a higher elevation.

The spacious public rooms are open to the outdoors. In the late afternoon, guests gather in the Sunset Lounge to relax with a drink, listen to a trio play gentle Hawaiian music, and watch the sun work its magic. Precisely at sunset, native drums start to throb and runners dash through the garden lighting the torchlamps with their torches. Suddenly all the lure of the islands is in the air and one is, curiously, both excited and absolutely at peace.

149

An opakapaka, a cousin of the red snapper, is presented in all its glory (overleaf). Fresh Pacific fish is a feature of the cuisine at this world-class resort.
Mauna Kea rises above one of the most beautiful beaches in the islands (left). A tribal carving of the head of a warrior echoes Hawaii's primitive past

MAUNA KEA BEACH HOTEL

Shortly after Hawaii became a state in 1959, Laurance S. Rockefeller was asked by island government and business leaders to help them increase tourism by creating a new vacation destination area. He toured the islands and found a site he loved on Kaunaoa Bay on the Big Island's sunny western side. Just north of the desolate black lava fields, it had a wide sandy beach, a rambling hillside, and commanded a breathtaking view of the Kohala Mountains and Mauna Kea, the extinct volcano that, if measured from the ocean floor, would be the highest mountain in the world at 32,000 feet.

Mr. Rockefeller commissioned Skidmore, Owings & Merrill to design his hotel. What the architects gave him was one of the most brilliant modern hotels in the world, perfectly suited to its task and its surroundings. Three levels of bedrooms step back as the structure rises to create private balconies for each room. The tiers do not meet and the center is open to the sky, tall palms rising from the garden court to the uppermost floor, and galleries overlooking the garden court. There is an interweaving of spaces, of indoors and out, that presents a constant series of delightful visual surprises. The gardens are equally stunning. The landscape architects—Belt, Collins & Associates, Ltd.—imported more than a half-million plants of some 200 varieties from other islands for the landscaping. In front, the gardens set the stage dramatically for one's first glimpse of the hotel; to the rear, they strikingly and logically, link the hotel to the beach and rocky shore.

Creating Mauna Kea brought out the perfectionist in Mr. Rockefeller. One example will suffice: throughout the lower level the flooring is a particularly lovely slate with unusual white traceries running through its blue-black surface. Mr. Rockefeller made it a condition of purchase that the small Mexican slate mine be flooded after his order was completed, so that no other hotel could have slate like his.

A guest at Mauna Kea does not have the feeling that he is in an Hawaiian resort, per se. This is deliberate. For inspiration, the creators drew on the culture of countries throughout the Pacific Basin, particularly Japan. The guest rooms, though luxurious, have the simplicity and linear quality one associates with Japan, an impression enhanced by a blue-and-white *yukata*, a Japanese cotton summer kimono, that is provided for each guest. The few pieces of furniture are simple and elegant of line. The absence of a television set seems perfectly natural.

A meticulous attention to detail is everywhere. Each guest is greeted with a lei. A small perfect orchid is on the pillow of the turned-down bed each night. There is an elaborate guest-history program listing each guest's individual requirements. If a guest requested a bedboard on his first visit, one will be in place when he returns. If he was on a salt-free diet, there will be no need to repeat the request. Understandably, most social guests do return.

One of the most delightfully unusual aspects of Mauna Kea is its collection of Asian and Pacific art, more than 1,000 pieces, most of them of museum quality. All are on view in the public spaces and around the grounds. A well-prepared booklet is in the guest rooms and with it one can take a leisurely and enlightening self-guided tour. In the North Garden, for example, is a prized piece: a five-foot-three-inch Indian Buddha carved from pink granite, placed on a pedestal so that, in accordance with Buddhist tradition, his heart is above the level of man's eye. (A tree that had been faring badly was transplanted next to the Buddha and now is thriving.) In the lobby are two *Mokala*, bronze statues of seated

Accuracy is a must
to clear the surf
and land on the
well-trapped green
(far left).
Arriving on an
American Airlines
Flagship the
islands seem like
jewels in the sea
(left). The warm
Pacific waters
lure a young guest
(below). The more
adventurous find
other challenges.
(bottom).

A feast fit for royalty is displayed by the Mauna Kea master chefs (left). A popular resident at the resort is a colorful parrot (below) who makes his home in a cage off the lobby. Throughout the public areas of the hotel is displayed a museum quality collection of art and handicrafts from Hawaii and the countries of the Pacific Basin.

disciples of Buddha, to welcome guests and guard the serenity of the hotel, much as they guarded the temples in Thailand where they were cast in the 19th Century. There are Japanese lacquered screens, tapas from Fiji, Thai guardian dogs, Maori carvings, Ceylonese batiks, and New Guinean war shields.

A collection of thirty Hawaiian quilts is displayed as wall hangings along the guest-room-floor galleries. The quilts were created expressly for Mauna Kea under the direction of Mealii Kalama, Hawaii's foremost quilter. In traditional island fashion, the patterns are cut free and they tell a story of Hawaii—her fruits, flowers, leaves, marine life, landmarks and legends. Each quilt has more than two million hand stiches and represents some one-thousand hours of work.

Art also enriches the resort's dining rooms. Two large Japanese *koi* (carp) greet guests in the Dining Pavilion. A collection of Pacifica food implements are on display in the Garden Pavilion. The wall hangings from Sri Lanka in the Batik Room are decorated with peacocks, parrots, elephants, butterflies and flowers. The Dining Pavilion and the more intimate Garden Pavilion are served by the same kitchen and have identical menus. One dines very well here, and only a sense of gastronomic adventure would lead a guest to the pleasures of the Batik Room. Executive Chef Kim Dietrich's menu entrees range from fish supplied daily by local fisherman to Pacific lobster and Chateaubriand. Salads with Waimea lettuce and special Camembert dressing, and spoom, sherbet splashed with champagne, are interim delights before sampling from the dessert cart. The wine list is well chosen and properly priced. There is a bountiful luncheon buffet daily, offering some 180 items in the Cafe Terrace. Guests at the beach or golf course can lunch at the Hau Tree Terrace of the 19th hole. At any meal, the Kona coffee is a treat all by itself.

The 7,016-yard, par-72 Mauna Kea course may well be the crowning masterpiece of Robert Trent Jones, Sr. Volcanic rock has been crushed fine and mixed with topsoil to produce a thick grassy course. From the second tee, one can see all three of the big volcanic peaks: Mauna Kea, Mauna Loa, and Halekala on Maui. The most famous hole is the third where one hits across a wave-tossed sea cove. The green tilts sharply toward the ocean, and one must hit to the right of the pin or be in trouble. The course is a constant challenge, particularly on windy days, and first-time players invariably score high.

Two tennis courts are tucked into the hillside near the Beachfront Wing, and there is 13-acre tennis park with another seven all-weather courts. The beach is spectacular; the water is calm in the summer and ideal for surfing in the winter. Guests may go bird hunting on the adjacent 227,000-acre Parker Ranch, the largest privately owned ranch in the United States, during the November-through-January season. Horses may be rented in Waimea, 12 miles away, and a variety of charter craft for deep-sea fishing. The resort owns a sleek 58-foot ocean-going Catamaran named Alii Nui (Great Chief) which it uses for snorkeling and scuba-diving trips and sunset sails.

There is a special, impromptu program at Mauna Kea on evenings when the sea is relatively calm. There is a walkway out to a rocky promontory where two powerful searchlights are trained on the water below. The light attracts the tiny sealife called plankton, and it in turn attracts manta rays which feed on it. The mantas, some measuring up to 20 feet, spread their huge wings and soar through the surf. Then they dart beneath the foam and reappear on the next wave. It's a most unusual performance and a memorable one.

Later, walking under the stars on the beach, the lights blinking in the hotel, one can readily understand why *Esquire* magazine once termed Mauna Kea "the greatest resort in the world."

THE RESORTS

ARIZONA BILTMORE,
24th Street at Missouri Avenue, Phoenix, Arizona 85016, (602) 955-6600, (800) 228-3000. 505 rooms. Rates: mid-September-May, single $130-$185, double $145-$200, one additional person $20, rates lower rest of year. Modified American Plan and various packages available. Check out noon, check in 4 p.m. Credit cards: American Express, Carte Blanche, Diners Club, Visa, MasterCard. Greens fees on two 18-hole courses from $11 to $25. Transportation available to Phoenix International Airport.

AUBERGE GRAY ROCKS,
Saint Jovite, Quebec, Canada JOT 2HO; (819) 425-2771, Montreal (514) 861-0187. 107 rooms in inn, 18 chalet suites, 39 deluxe rooms, 11 cottages. Rates: single, $78-$101, two or more, $319.50-$379, weekend rates, holiday weeks higher, various packages. American Plan. Credit cards: American Express, Carte Blanche, Diner's Club, Visa, MasterCard. Children's program; Green fees on 18-hole course, $9-$18; Check out, 2 p.m. The resort is located on Highway 327, 4 miles north of 117. Saint Jovite is served by International Montreal and Mirabelle Airports. (All prices Canadian dollars.)

THE BALSAMS,
Dixville Notch, New Hampshire 03576, (603) 255-3400, New York: (212) 563-4363, Boston (617) 227-8288. 232 rooms. Summer season: mid-May-mid-Oct. winter season: late December-late March. Rates: single, $86-$95, double, $72-$94, family rates. American Plan, summer; Modified American Plan, winter. Credit cards: American Express, Visa, MasterCard. Children's program, July-August; nursery service, winter. Crib, cot available. Check out noon, check in 3 p.m.; Airport and bus depot transportation. The resort is located on Rte. 26. There is no airport close to Dixville Notch.

BOCA RATON HOTEL AND CLUB,
Camino Real, Boca Raton, Florida 33432, (305) 395-3000, (800) 327-0101. 792 rooms. Rates: January-May, single $170-$270, double $190-$295, each additional person $45, Modified American Plan, lower rates rest of year, various packages available. Credit cards: American Express, Carte Blanche, Diners Club, Visa, MasterCard. Check out noon. Four 18-hole golf courses. Limousine service to West Palm Beach, Ft. Lauderdale and Miami airports. The hotel is between US 1 and A1A.

THE BREAKERS,
Palm Beach, Florida 33480, (305) 659-8440, Telex: 80-3414. 567 rooms. Rates: December-April, single $175-$270, double $185-$275, parlors $110-$225 additional; Modified American Plan; rates less rest of year, service charge added of $13 per single room, $16 double room; Credit cards: Visa, MasterCard; Check out noon, check in two p.m. Greens fee for 36-hole course $17. Transportation to West Palm Beach airport. The hotel is on South County Road, six blocks northeast on Rte. A1A, five miles east of I-95 Okeechobee Exit.

THE BROADMOOR,
Colorado Springs, Colorado 80901, (303) 634-7711. 560 rooms. Rates: May-early November, single or double $115-$155, each additional person $5, lower rates rest of year. Credit cards: Broadmoor Card only. Greens fee for two 18-hole courses $14 to $22 depending on season. Transportation to Colorado Springs and Denver airports. To reach hotel drive south five miles on Rtes. 85 and 87, then one mile west on Rte. 122.

CAMELBACK INN,
Box 70, 5402 East Lincoln Drive, Scottsdale, Arizona 85252, (602) 948-1700. 413 rooms. Rates: January-late May, single or double $150-$185, each additional person $10; American Plan $40 additional per person, lower rates rest of year. Modified American Plan $30.25, Camelback Plan (breakfast, lunch) $17.50, family rates in summer. Credit cards: American Express, Carte Blanche, Diners Club, Visa, MasterCard. Greens fees on two 18-hole courses $32.55. Transportation available to Phoenix International Airport. The Inn is four miles northwest of Scottsdale.

THE CLOISTER,
Sea Island, Georgia 31561, (912) 638-3611, (800) 841-3223. 264 rooms in hotel and villas, 320 in rental homes. Rates: March-late May, single, $115-$235, double, $140-$270, each additional person over 12 years of age, $35, six-12 years, $26; two to six, $18, less rest of year, monthly rates on cottages, sports and honeymoon packages available. American Plan. No credit cards. Greens fee for 54-hole courses $22, carts required, $12; The Cloister is serviced by the airports at Jacksonville, Florida, 70 miles away, and Savannah, Georgia, 80 miles away; car rentals are available or The Cloister will meet guests if notified in advance. The resort is located nine miles east of US 17, at Brunswick.

DORAL COUNTRY CLUB,
4400 NW 87 Avenue, Miami, Florida 33166, (305) 592-2000, (800) 327-6334. 652 rooms. Rates: mid-December-April, single or double $92-$142, each additional person $15. Modified American Plan available at $20 per person additional, lower rates rest of year, various packages available. Credit cards: American Express, Carte Blanche, Diners Club, Visa, MasterCard. Free transportation to Doral-on-the-Ocean and use of its facilities. No greens fees on four 18-hole courses. Transportation to Miami International Airport and railroad station. The hotel is eight miles northwest of Miami, a half-mile west of Rte. 826.

DORAL HOTEL-ON-THE-OCEAN,
4833 Collins Avenue, Miami Beach, Florida 33140, (305) 532-3600, (800) 327-6334. 420 rooms. Rates: mid-December-April, single or double $115-$130, each additional person $20. Lower rates rest of year, golf package available. European Plan. Credit cards: American Express, Carte Blanche, Diners Club, Visa, MasterCard. Free transportation to Doral Country Club and use of its facilities. Transportation to Miami International Airport and railroad station. The hotel is three miles north of Miami Beach on Rte. A1A.

GRAND HOTEL,

Mackinac Island, Michigan 49757, (906) 847-3331. 262 rooms. Season: Mid-May-November. Rates: single, $130, double, $165-$290, each additional person, $47.50, family rates available, 18 per cent service charge. Modified American Plan. No credit cards. Greens fee for nine-hole course $7. Mackinac Island is serviced by passenger ferries from Mackinaw City and St. Ignace, Michigan. No automobiles are allowed on the island. The Grand Hotel is six blocks from the dock, guests are picked up by horse-drawn carriage; Mackinac Island is served by the Pellston, Michigan, airport, 12 miles from the Mackinaw City ferry docks, where daily commerical flights connect with Detroit and Chicago.

GRAND HOTEL,

Point Clear, Alabama 36564, (205) 928-9201. 172 rooms in hotel, Bay House and cottages. Rates: $58-$102 per room European Plan, Modified American Plan available at $24 per person additional. Credit cards: American Express, Diners Club, Visa, MasterCard. Greens fees for 27-hole course $15, 18 holes $8.50. Transportation available to Mobile airport; The hotel is 23 miles southeast of Mobile on US 98, off I-10.

THE GREENBRIER,

White Sulphur Springs, West Virginia 24986, (304) 536-1110, (800) 624-6070. 700 rooms, 48 cottages. Rates: April to October, single, $118-$226; double, $94-$123 each, cottage with kitchen, $117-$165, rest of year lower rates, various packages available. Modified American Plan. Credit cards: American Express, Visa, MasterCard. Greens fees on three 18-hole courses $19. Private airport serviced by Piedmont. The resort is 1½ miles west of White Sulphur Springs on Rte. 60.

HARRAH'S HOTEL AND CASINO,

Box 8, Stateline, Nevada 89449, (702) 588-6611, (800) 648-5070. 536 rooms. Rates: May-October, single or double $85-$125, each additional person $15, rates vary rest of year; ski package available. Credit cards: American Express, Carte Blanche, Diners Club, Visa, MasterCard. Guests play golf on nearby public courses. Transportation available to Reno Airport. The resort is located on U.S. 50.

THE HOMESTEAD,

Hot Springs, Virginia 24445, (703) 839-5500. 589 rooms, 11 cottages. Rates: single, $100-$180, double, $96-$123, per person, parlor $55-$100 additional, cottage, four persons $419, various sports packages available; American Plan. No credit cards. Greens fees on three 18-hole courses $19. On Rte. 220; Daily flights to Washington D.C., from Ingalls Field by Colgan Airways; and Piedmont Airlines flights to nearby Roanoke, Virginia, or Lewisburg, West Virginia.

HOTEL DEL CORONADO,

1500 Orange Avenue, Coronado, California 92118, (619) 435-6611. 318 rooms in hotel, 208 in Ocean Towers and 96 in Poolside. Rates: single or double $68-$214, European Plan. Credit cards: American Express, Carte Blanche, Diners Club, Visa, MasterCard. Guests use nearby public golf course. Transportation available to San Diego airport; The hotel is just across the San Diego-Coronado Bridge, four miles southwest of I-5.

HOTEL HERSHEY,

Hershey, Pennsylvania 17033, (717) 533-2171. 250 rooms. Rates: single, $95-$101, double, $138-$143, suites, $178-$343, various sports packages, rest of year lower rates. Crib, cot free. April-November, Modified American Plan. Credit cards: American Express, Diners Club, Visa, MasterCard. Greens fee on nine-hole course, $7.50. Free airport, railroad station and bus depot transportation. 1½ miles north of US 322, Hershey is served by the Harrisburg International Airport.

INN OF THE MOUNTAIN GODS,

Box 259, Mescalero, New Mexico 88340, (505) 257-5141. 250 rooms. Rates: May-September, single or double $95, each additional person $8, rates lower rest of year, various sports packages available. Check out noon, check in 4 p.m. Credit cards: American Express, Carte Blanche, Diners Club, Visa, MasterCard. Greens fee for 18-hole course $17. Transportation available to Alamogordo Airport. The inn is on the Mescalero Apache Reservation, three miles southwest of Ruidoso and three miles north of Rte. 70.

INNISBROOK,

P.O. Drawer 1088, Tarpon Springs, Florida 33589; (813) 937-3124. 1,223 rooms in 25 lodges. Rates: mid-January-April, single or double $111, kitchen units $131-$151, various packages available, rates lower rest of year. American Plan, Modified American Plan. Credit cards: American Express, Carte Blanche, Diners Club, Visa, MasterCard. Greens fee on three 18-hole golf courses $16. Transportation available to Tampa International Airport and railroad station. The resort is one mile southeast of Tarpon Springs on Rte. 19.

LA COSTA HOTEL AND SPA,

Costa Del Mar Road, Carlsbad, California 92008, (714) 438-9111, Telex 697-946. 320 rooms. Rates: single or double $125-$150. European Plan; spa and various sports packages available. Credit cards: American Express, Visa, MasterCard. Greens fee for 27-hole course $25. Transportation available to San Diego Airport. From I-5 take La Costa Avenue exit to El Camino Real, left to entrance.

THE LODGE AT PEBBLE BEACH,

Pebble Beach, California 93953, (408) 624-3811. 161 rooms. Rates: single or double $150-$160. European Plan only. Check out 2 p.m., check in 4 p.m. Credit cards: American Express, Carte Blanche, Diners Club, Visa, MasterCard. Greens fees for two 18-hole courses $40-$75 including cart. Transportation available to Monterey airport. The resort is three miles north of Carmel on 17-Mile Drive.

MAUNA KEA BEACH HOTEL,
Kamuela, Hawaii 96743, (808) 882-7222, (800) 228-3000, Canada (800) 268-8383 (in Toronto (800) 368-4684), Alaska and Hawaii (800) 228-1212, Telex 743-822-7090. 310 rooms; Rates: single $215-$285, double $230-$300, additional person in room $60, various packages available. Modified American Plan. No credit cards. No greens fee on 18-hole course. Transportation to airport at Kona; Aloha Airlines and other inter-island carries service Kona from Honolulu and other islands. United Airlines flies direct to Hilo Airport from Mainland U.S.

PINEHURST ,
Box 4000, Pinehurst, North Carolina 28378, (919) 295-6811, (800) 334-9553. 270 rooms, 310 1-3 bedroom villas. Rates: mid-March-late May, and early-September-mid-November, single, $112, double, $150, suites, $105 per person, villas, $150-$330, lower rest of year, golf and tennis packages available, 15 per cent service charge. Modified American Plan. Credit Cards: American Express, Diners Club, Visa, and MasterCard. Greens fees for six 18-hole courses $25. Airport transportation available; Pinehurst is serviced by Eastern, United and Piedmont through airports at Raleigh/Durham, Fayetteville or Charlotte. Mid-South Aviation has daily flights from Raleigh/Durham to Moore County Airport, seven miles from Pinehurst. The resort is located just west of village on Rte. 5, 1½ miles west of US 15.

THE PINES ,
Box 70, Digby Bay, Nova Scotia, Canada B0V 1A0; (902) 245-2511; Telex 019-32186. 89 rooms in hotel, 30 1-3 bedroom cottages. Season: May-October; Rates: single, $37-$61, double, $50-$98, cottages, $10-$34. Modified American and European plans. Credit cards: American Express, Visa, MasterCard. The resort is 1 mile north of Digby Bay on Shore Road. Greens fee on 18-hole course, $10. Daily car-ferry service between Digby Bay and Saint John, New Brunswick. Air service to Halifax and Yarmouth; private aircraft at Digby Bay airport.

RANCHO LAS PALMAS ,
41000 Bob Hope Drive, Rancho Mirage, California 92270, (619) 568-2727. 456 rooms. Rates: late-December-mid-May, single or double $135-$155, each additional person $10 and up, rates lower rest of year. American and Modified American Plans, family rates and various packages available. Credit cards: American Express, Carte Blanche, Diners Club, Visa, MasterCard. Greens fee on 27-hole course $13-$23 depending on season. Free transportation to Palm Springs Airport. The resort is 12 miles south of Palm Springs.

SEA PINES PLANTATION,
Hilton Head Island, South Carolina 29928, (803) 785-3333, (800) 845-6131. 202 rooms including 28 cottage suites (hotel), 800 units in villas, and 125 homes (plantation). Rates: hotel, March-October, single and double, $80-$125, cottage suites, $150, lower rates rest of year, plantation villas, $105-$255 for one to four bedrooms. Sports packages available. European plan. Credit cards: American Express, Diners Club, Visa, MasterCard. Greens fees for three 18-hole courses, $18-$26. Both hotel and plantation are on Rte. 278. Sea Pines Plantation is 43 miles from Savannah, Georgia, and 95 from Charleston, South Carolina, both cities serviced by Delta and Eastern Airlines. Southbound motorists exit Interstate 95 to Rte. 462 to 170 and 278 to the island.

SUN VALLEY,
Sun Valley Road, Sun Valley, Idaho 83353, (208) 622-4111. 265 rooms in the Lodge and Inn, 112 in the condominiums. Rates: single or double $51-$160, each additional person $8. Lower rates. April-May and October-mid-December. Credit cards: American Express, Visa, MasterCard. Greens fee for 18-hole course $21. Transportation available to Hailey Airport, where scheduled commuter lines fly to Salt Lake City, Utah, and Boise, Idaho. The resort is one mile east of Ketchum.

WESTIN WAILEA BEACH,
Box 689, Wailea, Maui, Hawaii 96573, (808) 879-4900, Canada (800) 365-8383 (in Toronto (800) 365-7700), Alaska and Hawaii (800) 228-1212, Telex 708-8799107. 350 rooms. Rates: mid-December to March, single or double $105-$180, third person in room $15, European Plan (Modified American Plan available at extra cost), most rates lower rest of year, family rates and various packages available. Credit cards: American Express, Diners Club, Visa, MasterCard. Greens fee $25 for two 18-hole golf courses. Transportation to Kahului Airport. Aloha Airlines and other inter-island carriers service Kahului.

THE WIGWAM,
Litchfield and Indian School Roads, Litchfield Park, Arizona 85340, (602) 935-3811. 220 rooms in 38 cottages. Season: September-May. Rates: single $116-$156 double, per person $72-$92, each additional person $28, parlor $56 additional, family rates and various packages available. American Plan. No credit cards. Greens fees for three 18-hole golf courses $17. Transportation to Phoenix International Airport. The resort is 2½ miles north of I-10.

ACKNOWLEDGMENTS

Visiting all the great resorts and photographing them would
have been a longer, harder and less enjoyable task but for
my associate, George Wieser, Jr. His skill, energy and unflagging
good spirits were most appreciated. Special thanks to American
Airlines for flying us to Hawaii, and to Aloha Airlines for flying
us around the islands. The resorts themselves were charming,
hospitable and cooperative. Certain photographs were supplied by
the individual resorts. They appear as follows:
page 16 (lower left), pages 112-113, page 115, page 116, page 117
(bottom), page 121, and page 139 (lower left and upper right).
The bottom photograph on page 97 is by George Wieser, Jr.